Stock Market Investing for Beginners

The Complete Guide to Generate
Passive Income with Simple Trading
Strategies, Start Creating Your
Wealth and Financial Freedom with
Proven Strategies

Jim Douglas

for any reparation, damages, or monetary loss due to the information herein, either directly or indirectly.

Respective authors own all copyrights not held by the publisher.

The information herein is offered for informational purposes solely, and is universal as so. The presentation of the information is without contract or any type of guarantee assurance.

The trademarks that are used are without any consent, and the publication of the trademark is without permission or backing by the trademark owner. All trademarks and brands within this book are for clarifying purposes only and are the owned by the owners themselves, not affiliated with this document.

Table of Contents

Introduction

You may have heard words such as stock market and stock trading before. However, you are not exactly sure what they mean. They are simply words that mean money and investment to you. This chapter, however, demystifies the ideas you may have about stock trading and the stock market. By the end of the chapter, you will have a clear understanding of what the stock market is and how it works. Read on for more.

If you are wondering how the stock market works, then read on as I explain.

Understanding how the stock market works is not difficult. Think of it like an auction house, where buyers and sellers negotiate prices and find the best compromise before making a trade. The only aspect that differentiates the stock market from an auction house is the fact that the latter works through a network of exchanges. Take the example of the popular NASDAQ or New York Stock Exchange. A company will list its stocks' shares on an exchange in a process commonly known as IPO- an initial public offering. As an investor, you would purchase the shares, and the company you buy from will get the chance to raise money for their business.

On the other hand, you are free to buy and sell these stocks among other investors like you. The exchange plays a vital role in tracking the demand and supply of the different stocks, so you have all the necessary resources you need to trade. The willingness of the investors and traders to buy and sell-supply and demand- helps determine the price of each of the securities. It gets a bit complex here because computer algorithms are involved in doing the calculations.

The process of buying and selling begins with the buyers offering a bid-the highest amount they can pay, or are willing to pay. Normally, the bid is usually a lower price than that set by the sellers. This difference has a term, the bid-ask spread. For a trade to be successful, one of the two parties involved in the exchange has to budge. That means that the seller has to lower his price or the buyer has to increase his bid or price.

While it is likely that stock trades took place in physical marketplaces before the arrival of the internet, this trade today is done electronically. There are two platforms, online stockbrokers and the internet. The trade happens on a stock by stock basis, but often, you find that the stock prices move simultaneously because they are all affected by similar political events, news, and economic reports.

You may probably be wondering how to best invest in the stock market. However, if you are working and you have a 401(k) plan, there is a chance you have already invested in the stock market. The 401(k) plan usually has mutual funds, which is a composition of stocks from different companies. Alternatively, you can purchase stocks through an individual retirement account or a brokerage account. Opening both accounts can be done through online brokers, and you can as well buy and sell investments. These online brokers act as middlemen between stock exchanges and people who buy stocks like you.

What you need to know as you begin your trading journey is that stock trading is an investment like any other. However, it carries more risk than a standard investment and has the potential to offer you more return as well in comparison to other securities. There are some smart alternatives that as an individual, you can consider while stock trading to avoid purchasing many different funds. For example, you can invest in an exchange-traded fund or index fund. The exchange-traded and index funds mirror the performance of a specific index by holding all the investments and stocks in the index.

Most importantly, you should remember that stock trading is best done as a long-term investment solution. It cannot be an option for short-term investment because if you consider it a short term investment, there is likelihood that you may need your money back before the end of the short term period. It is exceedingly difficult to recover your money in case the market suffered losses.

Chapter 1: How to Get Started with Stocks

There are many different methods that you can use in order to help you invest your money. Some may include working with the forex market and trading currencies. Some may include getting into real estate and flipping homes or becoming a landlord. You may start your own business, invest in a retirement plan, and so much more. But one method that you may want to check out when getting started in investing is the stock market.

No matter what reason you choose to go with to invest, getting started with the stock market as your vehicle of investing can be an easy choice. The stock market can provide you with a lot of options when it comes to what you want to invest in. You can choose to have a more conservative plan, or you can choose to take on more risk, and many traders fall somewhere in between. While you must look through the different options and determine which one is right for you, you will quickly find that the stock market has everything you need to be successful.

Basic of Stock Market

If you want to multiply your money and grow wealth, the secret lies in saving and investing. When it comes to investing, there are many ways to do it. You could put your money in stocks, bonds, commodities, real estate, cash equivalents, precious metals, peer-to-peer lending, the list is endless. Among this, however, stocks are among one of the best investment options. Below are some reasons why you should invest in stocks.

Stock trading information

Whenever you read any kind of stock investment guide or book, it's too easy to just get beaten up by all the jargon. It's too easy to get clobbered by all the technical terms. I'm going to spare you of all of that by speaking in plain English.

I'll try to strip down these terms into their simplest forms so not only can you understand them more quickly, but you would be able to relate these concepts to each other. This increases the likelihood that you would not be intimidated by stock trading.

This is one common problem that I see over and over again. A lot of people who'd like to go into stock trading and investing get intimidated because they think that it's all technical, that they're in way over their head. In fact, they get so scared that they feel that they're just basically going to lose money, hand over fist.

That doesn't have to be the case and stripping down the terms into easy to understand forms can go a long way in making you less intimated. The less intimidated you are, the more your curiosity can take over and you can learn what you need to learn to do a good job in trading with a constant level of success.

Bull markets vs. bear markets

Each investor has a different opinion about the whole economy or the stock markets. The buyers and sellers have different expectations about trading in the stock market. When there is optimism about trading and the prices increase, it is called the bull market and when the prices increases due to lacks of optimists the market is said to be bear market.

The bull market is a kind of market in which there is less unemployment; more people get the jobs, the economy of the country increases and the stock prices also rise. It is easy to trade in a bull market because the prices are getting high. A bull is a person who his optimistic about the stocks and believes that the costs of the shares will increase. However, the bull market is temporary send cannot last forever as it is because there will be a time when this market will also go down.

On the other hand, the bear market is the opposite of the bull market. A bear market is said to be the market when unemployment increases in the country or the economy falls. It makes the in esters to think for a long time whether they should invest in the market or not. They usually wait until they see that bear market is almost to its end and the bull market is rising soon.

Stock market crash vs. correction

When it comes to the stock market, this knowledge seems to go out the window. Of course, you will not find a Christmas season or Black Friday sale on the stock market. Sales in the stock market refer to times when stocks are going at relatively low prices. Unfortunately, when prices go low, instead of buying, most investors get nervous and keep away from these stocks. However, this is the best time to buy stocks. Good examples of sales in the stock market include the period following a market crash (note: just *after* the crash, not during the crash), or the period following a market correction. During such periods, you can easily get valuable stocks at a bargain.

As a stock trader, you should not buy stocks blindly. Before you decide to purchase, you should have a price in mind that you are willing to purchase the stock at. This should be a price that you feel the stock is capable of rising above, allowing you to make a profit. You should then wait for the stock to hit this price, at which point you can purchase the stock and wait for the price to rise again. Of course, your target buy price needs to be realistic, or else the share price might never get to your buy price. It's also good to think of your target buy price as a range, rather than a specific price point.

The importance of diversification

People who are keeping the investment products on another end will have to get through the stock market investing which will be there for the diversifications over the time of providing them benefit. It helps in the stock market and the value change for the individual with getting different types of investment such as real estate and the bonds. When you have a stock, it helps in the losses compared to the products which are related to finances. These types of portfolios can be beneficial for the significant and rapid gains which the investors want along with the risk of adopting different kinds of strategies for investment. It helps them to avoid the risk which they are taking with having the plan which is conservative on the other end.

Chapter 2: Reason to Begin Investing in Stock Market

There are several reasons why investors purchase stocks. Here are some of the following:

Capital Appreciation

They want to get the capital appreciation which can occur when the price of the stock rises. Another reason is dividend payments when it comes to distributing the company's earning within the stockholders. They can also be bought for the vote sharing or to influence another company. Every investor has their reasons to buy stocks, yet they are beneficial on both sides, for the investor and the stock market itself.

Generating Money

Companies issue stocks to get money for numerous things like when they have to pay off the dent, expand their business in new markets, build new facilities, bring new equipment or launch new products. Anything which may bring them more profit will be a reason why they would want to issue the stocks so they can get money for investment.

How to invest

When you are investing in stocks, there are specific strategies which you have to adapt to be successful. There is a complete study over it then you can make the mind and decision of investing your money into something which will bring you some positive results out of it. You can spend the entire life to deal with the single stock or work through it without figuring out how it works. You have to understand the investment potential to get good results and the rewards it gives to the people who are working over it.

For the people who are investing in the stocks for the first time, it may be their biggest concern that they will lose everything and it will be significant. It is a fear which is in the brain of every investor when they have to get their feet into the stocks. Well, you invest into the mutual funds and then get the access to the shares in a different way with coming through the diversification along with eh broad-based mutual funds which are the primary security measurement to keep it simple for you. You have to look at the entire market to know that if the company gets hurt then, there will be a significant impact over the portfolio overall. The individual stocks are there for the more rewarding meaning keeping it clear for the shareholders to deal with the ongoing market trends. When there are individual stocks, then it needs to have the diversified mutual funds which are helpful for you to pick the right ones and carry on with it.

Selling Your Stocks

When you learned to drive, you didn't just jump in the car and turn it on. Instead, someone walked you through exactly what to do before you started the car. You were told what the stick-shift or automatic PRNDL was for. You were told how to move the mirrors, what was forward and reverse, and other buttons in the car. Before you invest in the stock market, you need to walk, not run. You need a guide that tells you how things work, so you avoid making costly mistakes. As long as you know how something works, you don't have to be afraid of the reality of it.

Many people do not understand investing, so the stock market scares them. The reality is—you just need to know how it works, the parts that make it work, and you can set up an investment strategy that works.

A stock is usually referred to as a share. It is a share in a company that is looking for investors. These investors provide capital for the company to grow the company. When a company first offers shares it is called an IPO or Initial Public Offering. The share price is set on the estimated worth of the company, as well as the number of shares available for sale.

For the shares to be publicly offered, a company needs to be listed on a stock exchange, like the NYSE. Traders and investors can then buy and sell stocks, but the company will only make money with the IPO. After the IPO is over, it is simply businessmen, individuals, and investors trading the stocks between themselves to make a profit and dividends.

Chapter 3: Stock Market News and Media

For lots of years, institutional investors have garnered valuable information about investment, but now you can take out your cell phone, open mobile applications of a company, and collect the information you need about the daily position of the stock market. Technology has revolutionized the way information is processed. Major newspapers carry a minimum of stock price tables in the business sections. They never offer advice or recommendations for investors. However, they do provide daily news about the economic situation and also an understanding of financial options for investors and for the people who are seeking a career in the brokerage profession.

How News Affects Stock Prices

The most important column of the business daily is the section that carries trade volume separately for each company. Most newspapers carry details of the per day volume of a particular stock and some of them carry details of the trading volume of a particular company for the past three months. They show records of the normal trading level. Every stock is different in its trading volume and price. It is highly probable and normal that one stock trades 10,000 shares a day, while the other one trades 100,000 per day. Some of them cross 1 million shares a day in trade volume.

If a stock had the average trading volume of 10,000 shares per day, but it starts transacting 70,000 per day, and its price jumps one point, the stock has recorded a 600% increase in its volume. That's humongous, to say the least. You can easily see that the newspaper had entered +600 in the points column for trade volume. That's how you can analyze the position of every stock on the go. All you have to do is open your cell phone application, skim through the finance section of the business daily, and enter it in your red diary. Once this becomes your daily practice, you can do the daily math you need to develop a winning strategy. You can easily tell which stock has the potential to become the leader and which one the laggard.

This, no doubt, is essential data to sift through and keep with you. Just imagine the fact that the stock you hold posted 400% greater volume than normal over the past day. Isn't this news for you? Shouldn't you be aware of this brilliant development? This single reason is enough to read a business daily regularly and take notes in your diary. You need these calculations, data, and information for both long-term and short-term gains. The data allows you to scrutinize the flow of money in and out of stocks. Lots of sophisticated investors, as well as experienced stockbrokers, widely utilize this advanced news dissemination. You can find tables in the newspapers that allow you to skim through many companies in a single reading.

Chapter 4: Investing Strategies in Financial Markets

While it comes to the accumulation of wealth and personal finance, some subjects are a bit more talked as compared to stocks. It is simple to figure out why: playing with a stock market is quite thrilling. However, on the financial roller-coaster, everyone wants to experience some thrilling ups in the absence of downs.

There're nearly six-thousand traded firms in the United States. It shows a 37 percent decrease in the number of American-listed firms since 1997. What should an investor choose?

Tested Strategies

In the chapter, we will examine some most important time-tested strategies to find good stocks (at least trying to avoid bad ones). We will learn the stock-picking art relying on a specific set of criteria, to get a return rate that's above the market's average.

Some are easy: for instance, The Dogs of the Dow strategy is very easy that this takes a couple of minutes to understand how the whole system does work. Value investing and growth are quite complicated, and these kinds of investors need to invest time to understand financial ratios, valuation, to name a few.

The Basics of Growth Stock Investment Strategies

Patience is undoubtedly a virtue while this comes to investment – in terms of patiently waiting for the appropriate time for entering a position, and waiting for a while until you have done all of the homework before making your very first investment. The chances of success would enhance greatly when you know very well about what you are doing.

A lot of long-term investors generally use the fundamental analysis for finding out possible chances. When you are interested in understanding these methods, learn fundamental analysis that would teach you the tools and strategies used by the successful investment experts. You would learn how to analyze cash flow and income statements, spot weak points in a balance sheet of the stock, and also use different valuation ratios for comparing opportunities in different on-demand video, interactive content, and exercises.

A Fusion of Value and Growth

As the name implies, growth investors are more interested in a company's future than where they are at currently. So much so, that the current price of the company's stock barely factors into the equation at all. This strategy hinges on buying into companies that are currently trading at a point that is above their intrinsic value based on the belief that this value will continue growing to the point that it exceeds the current valuation.

In order to properly take advantage of this strategy, you are going to want to be on the lookout for younger companies that are much more likely to grow rapidly when compared to companies that are more well-established. This strategy hinges on the assumption that growth in revenue or earnings will directly translate into an increase in the underlying stock price. Other viable choices include companies whose industry is experiencing a rapid rate of expansion and those that are in fields related to new technological advancements. Profits are then realized not based on dividends but based on capital gains instead. These companies will rarely pay dividends at all due to the fact that profits are more often going to be reinvested back into the company instead.

Chapter 5: Stock Market Psychology

Before you decide to jump right into stock market investing, you must take some time to determine what your goals are for doing this kind of investing. If you jump into this investment without thinking it through, you will fail miserably. You should know where you want to start out at as well as why you are doing the investment. Do you want to start investing to help your retirement fund, to make a side income, or even to replace your full income? The answer to this will help determine how you will behave when you get into the market.

There are many options that you can choose for goals when you want to invest. Choosing the right one can sometimes help you to figure out how much risk you want to take and which stocks you want to invest in. For example, if you are looking to turn the stock market investment into your full-time income, you may be willing to take on more risk to bring in more money. If you want to make just enough to put some in the bank or pay off a few bills, then it may be best to go with less risky options.

No matter which goal you choose for investing, you will quickly find that the stock market is one of the best options that you can choose for your investment. There are many companies that you can choose to work with, many strategies that work well, and even different levels of risk that you can pick from. You can pick a plan that has a bit more risk that will also help you earn more rewards, or you can take your time to learn more about the stock market and pick less risky options while still making money.

You do need to have a good idea of how the stock market works and how to get into the game before you start. First, we need to understand what a stock is. A stock is a type of security that will give the investor, or you if you choose this option, part ownership in the business that the stock belongs to. This also means that the investor will be able to claim some of the assets and earnings of the business as well. The buyer will be known as a shareholder, and along with some of the other investors, they will be the new owners of that

24

business. The amount of ownership that you have will depend on a number of stocks that you possess. There are also two types of stocks including common stocks and preferred stocks.

The Bottom Line

One of the first questions that you may have as a new investor is how to trade stocks. When you join in on the stock market, you must trade stocks using the stock exchange. This is simply the place where the sellers and buyers of stocks will come together and then agree on the price for a particular stock. There are a few places where you can physically go to do this, but for the most part, you will do your trades online.

Once you get into the stock market and look at it for a bit, you will notice that the prices of each stock will change all the time. Many different factors come into play when determining what the price of the stock will be. These factors change on a regular basis, which is what makes it so hard to keep the prices steady for the long term. For example, if the supply of the stock is pretty high while the demand is low, the price of that stock will stay lower. If the demand for the particular stock goes up and the supply goes down or stays the same, then the price of those stocks will go up as well. The prices of the various stocks will usually be what people in the stock market see as the worth of the stocks and can show how interested people are in purchasing that stock at one time or another.

Not only can you pay attention to the demand and supply of a particular stock, but you will also find that the earnings of the company behind the stock can determine how much it is worth as well. This means that you need to look at how much money the company is able to earn each year. Of course, the exact amount will change from one year to another, so it is a good place to start to see if the company is growing and if you will be able to make some money from the investment. It is easy to find these numbers by looking through some of the financial journals and reports that the company is required to put out in order to be on the stock market.

Keeping track of all the prices on the stock market can be hard, and the fact that there are a lot of reasons that these stock prices will change can be a hassle as well. You have to look at some of the changes that the company has recently made or will make soon. Additionally, you need to look at how well the economy is doing at the time. What this all means is that you do need to do some research. Those who just jump right into the stock market and don't pay attention to what is going on around them are more likely to fail and lose a lot of money.

There is no rush when getting into the stock market. You can do this on your own time and do some thorough research to make sure you are picking out the right stocks and not just risking everything. Finding a good stockbroker to help you along the way can make the process so much easier as well.

Right Mindset

When it comes to investing your money and putting it to work for you, there are several opportunities that you can choose from. Each person has their own personal style when it comes to these investments and picking out the one that is best for their needs. Some people might like to get their hands dirty and follow the market with real estate investing. Some like to play it safe and will just put their money into a retirement plan. And others will choose to work with the stock market.

Often it will depend on how much time you have to devote to the investment, how much money you can put towards the investment, and how much risk you are willing to take. Of course, the more risk you are willing to take, the more money you could potentially make. There is also the risk of losing more money, which is why you need to find the perfect balance between how much you can earn with an investment and how much you could lose with that investment if things go wrong.

While there are a lot of different investment opportunities that you can choose from, such as real estate investing, investing in bonds, starting your own business and more, you can also work with the stock market. This type of investment will include you taking your money and investing it to help another company grow. In return for investing in a company that does well, you will earn dividends each quarter, or part of the profit that the company brings in. Or you could get into the process of buying the stocks at a lower price and selling them when the price goes up so that you can make a profit.

Those are the two most common ways to make money in the stock market, but there are many others that you can work with as well. With all the options available for investing in the stock market, it is no wonder that a lot of people choose to go with this option. You will be able to take a look at how much time, money, and risk you have available and choose which stocks, as well as which strategies, will be the best for you. Depending on which stocks you go with, it is even possible to start making a profit without all the wait.

It is exciting to get into the stock market and see how things can go for you, but some people want to weigh all their options and make sure that they can actually make money rather than losing out on money. When you are ready to start entering the stock market, and you want to make a good income from your investment, make sure to learn the right strategies that will ensure that you see success.

Chapter 6: How to Make Money In the Stock Market

While buying your first stock can be exciting, if you want to make money as a trader, you have to sell the stock. Here, the general rule of thumb is to buy low and sell high. While I mentioned above that buying at the right time increases the possibility of turning a profit, selling at the right time guarantees you that profit. If you sell at the wrong time, any advantages you had from buying at the right time are negated.

Selling your stocks can be a very emotionally charged affair. Even if you have already made a profit, deciding whether to take those profits or hold on to the stock in the hope that it will rise even higher can be a difficult call. If your position is already in loss, it can be equally difficult to decide whether to sell at that point and cut your losses or hold on to the stock in the hopes that it will reverse and allow you to recoup the money you have lost so far. Keep in mind, however, that holding on could potentially lead to even bigger losses. Below, let's take a look at how to sell your stocks.

Making money in stocks

The first step is to determine why you want to sell. As a trader, the top reason for selling should be that your stock has hit your target price. Before getting into a position, you should have determined the price at which you will sell the stock. Once your stocks hit your target sell price, you can sell, since you will already have made your targeted profits. Having a target price can prevent you from making emotionally charged decisions, such as holding onto a stock for too long, which can wipe out your profits (and potentially lead to loss) in case the prices reverse.

Another reason to sell is when you receive information showing that the company's fundamentals are showing signs of stress. If you notice this, any other negative signs might lead to a mass panic, which will, in turn, cause the share price to nosedive. In such cases, it is best to sell while you still have some profit.

Index funds or individual stocks?

While there are a variety of options that you can go with when you join the stock market, most beginners are going to choose between two types of investments they may work with a stock mutual fund or an exchange-traded fund, or they may work with individual stocks.

Index funds and ETFs track an index. For example, you can work with an S&P 500 fund that will replicate that index by buying the stock of the companies that are in that fund. When you decide to invest in one of these funds, you will own small parts of each company in the fund. You can also decide to have several of these funds to help you build up a strong and diversified portfolio to invest in.

The other option is to work with some individual stocks. If you want to invest in one specific company, you can choose to purchase a single share or several if you have the money. This is a good way to dip your toes into the water and see how it goes. Building a portfolio that is diversified with this option is possible, but it will take you more time because these are usually more expensive to purchase at the beginning.

The upside of going with the stock mutual funds is that they are set up to be diversified. This is a great way to lessen the amount of risk you are going to take on when you join the stock market. But it is very unlikely that you will see a huge rise in prices as you can sometimes see with individual stocks.

The upside of choosing to go with individual stocks is that a wise pick can earn you a big profit, but the odds that one stock will be able to make you rich are very slim. The risks are higher with this kind of option as well.

For those who are just getting started with the stock market, it is often best to go with the mutual funds. This helps you build up your portfolio and reduce your risks as things start to grow. You can always go with an individual stock after you have some time to grow your money and can take on more risks.

Chapter 7: Initial Public Offering (IPO)

A good definition of IPO is that the Initial Public Offering, an instrument governed by the law through which a company obtains the dissemination of its titles among the public. Using what is technically called the creation of the float, the company obtains the listing of its securities on the regulated market.

Some of these terms may seem difficult. For those who are just beginners we can say that the IPO is a solicitation to invest. Thus, the Initial Public Offering is a real invitation to invest. Having clarified the meaning of IPO let's move on.

How does the Initial Public Offer work? The legislative background of this application is represented by the Consolidated Law on Finance (Legislative Decree 58/1998). This law provides for a whole series of provisions on information and transparency. The indistinct public of the subjects potentially interested in the IPO (recipients of the offer) has the right to know all the useful information to decide whether to join the IPO in full awareness.

Understanding an IPO

The IPO process is decidedly long and complex. By regulation, the IPO foresees the involvement of a series of very different subjects. The following subjects participate in the various phases of the Initial Public Offering:

- the issuing company;

- the global coordinator;

- the sponsor;

- the specialist;

- the financial advisor;

- the law firms in charge; and

- the members of the placement consortium.

When one wonders how the IPO works, it should be noted that the first phase of the process is represented by the sending to SEC of the prior communication from the company concerned. The prior communication is an official document that the company presents to the SEC. The same company that aims to be listed on the stock exchange is responsible for drawing up the Prospectus according to the legal framework.

From what we have said, it is easy to deduce that an IPO can last even a month. If you then consider the whole procedure for admission to the stock market then you also get to 4 or even 6 months. In short, before betting on the performance of what's listed, one must allow quite a bit of time to pass. This prolonging, of course, also has an impact on the possibility of trading on the shares of that listed company.

Largest IPOs

In an IPO a business will typically sell two types of shares: primary and secondary. Technically there is no difference between these two types of shares. The difference only lies in their source. Though the financial requirements of the business are a strong motivation for going public, the sale of existing shares (secondary shares, owned by the owners of the business) does not affect the business financially – the proceeds from the sale of secondary shares go only to the owners of the shares. It is only the sale of newly created shares (primary shares) that bring money to the firm's accounts at the time of the IPO. As stated, most IPOs offer a mix of both primary and secondary shares.

The mix of primary and secondary shares being sold by a firm in an IPO is usually mentioned in the listing prospectus and can be revealing. For example, if all the shares on sale only come from the existing owners – they are all secondary shares – this would be alarming as it would signal a **cash in and run** from the owners.

A sector is a segment of the stock market that offers similar sets of markets and generally caters to the needs of the same market. It is a general category of companies that share a similar nature of business. The financial sector for example, may include banks, investment companies and lending companies. They all generally do business related to money.

When you are just starting out, you want to first study the sectors and subsectors that you are already familiar with. If you spend a lot of time reading about technology news for instance, you may already be familiar with many of the companies and the current events in the technology sector. You may even delve deeper in the Computer Manufacturing subsector. This is where you will see popular tech companies like Apple Inc. (AAPL), Dell Technologies Inc. (DVMT) and HP (HPE).

It will be faster and easier for you to learn about sectors that you are already familiar with and you are interested in. If you choose to learn about a sector that you are not familiar with, you may end up spending more time than necessary researching and reading about them. You may become stuck when you encounter industry jargons that are only known to those who are already in the industry.

If there is no one sector that you are already knowledgeable about, you could pick an industry that you are genuinely interested in. This way, learning will not be as hard because you enjoy reading about the industry.

You could also choose an industry where you participate as a consumer. If you spend a lot on clothes and apparels for instance, you could also choose to learn about the companies in the Clothing/Shoe/Accessory Stores subsector. This subsector is included in the Consumer Services sector and it includes some of the biggest clothing brands like Gap Inc. (GPS), Nike (NKE) and Nordstrom Inc. (JWN).

Underwriters and the IPO Process

When referring to this method for fixing the price of the offer on the stock exchange, the first question concerns the definition of book building. With this strange term, we indicate the process by which the application form of the institutional investors who have submitted an order concerning a security offer transaction is drafted. Through this process the price of the same securities is set.

The global coordinator manages this process. This figure has the task of collecting all the purchase / subscription orders of institutional investors in a book called the institutional book. Orders are collected based on price or time priority or size. Each order can be expressed in number of shares or in counter value. Finally, each order is linked to the price limit indicated by the originator. Through this process it is possible to draw a curve which shows the price of the IPO.

Chapter 8: Mutual Funds and How to Use Them

Most people who are unaware of mutual funds believe that it is a waste of time and money. Little do they know how big it is as an opportunity. There are four facets of mutual funds: the investor, the fund manager, and the trustee's monitor.

The investors are the people who give out their money to the mutual fund. This is where you belong as a start-up investor. The fund manager, preferably from Asset Management Companies (AMC), is likened to be an engineer or a doctor of mutual funds. From the name itself, he is responsible for managing your mutual funds and diversifying it into the market. To make sure that the assets maintain their value and grow profits, we have trustees who monitor the money in the market. The trustees also ensure the efficiency of the fund managers in putting the money into the market.

The Basics of a Mutual Fund

Starting a mutual fund is actually easier than other forms of investment vehicles. Because you have a manager to make sure your money generates interest. All you need to do is set a goal, and go from there. But we will discuss more of this later. Mutual funds are a form of investment where you literally sleep while you earn. You can leave it all to your fund manager and wait for ten years or so to become a millionaire. You heard that right! Depending on your investment, you can earn as much as millions. Of course, the bigger the investment, the bigger the income.

Now, why do you need to wait for ten years or so? Well, there are factors that influence the money market industry like the economy and inflation rate. Sometimes, calamities and other unexpected factors can also contribute to the rise and fall of the interest rate in the money market. If you look at the picture below, you can see the upward trend of the graph. Think of it as your money in the market. If you withdraw your funds in the first quarter of a ten-year plan, you will generate less income from your investment. Depending on the current interest rate, you might even incur a loss.

Which is why it is important to keep investing until you finish your desired plan. But what if I want to continue investing more money even after the ten-year plan? Then, you can choose not to withdraw your funds and go for more years of investing to generate a larger income. I am sure that there are options in the market for you so your investment will not be as heavy and you will have more room for your needs and miscellaneous expenses.

Investing in a mutual fund is like saving money. But unlike the typical way of saving, in mutual funds, your money actually generates income while it revolves in the market. If your goal is a safe and secure retirement, then you can be a millionaire by the time you turn 60 years old.

Mutual funds also offer short-term investments. For example, you want to earn for your future house and lot, car, and college tuition for your kids. There are plans that will offer you short-term investments to make ready for your upcoming milestones. Amazing, isn't it?

But before you invest in anything. You need to ensure the quality and reliability of your fund managers. You need to learn how to discriminate a bad investment from a good one. Times these days are full of scams. So, before you choose, do prior research on the company, bank, or corporation.

How Mutual Funds Work

Mutual funds are financial institutes whose purpose is to invest the funds raised by savers. The aim is to create value, through the management of a series of assets, for the fund managers and for the investors who have invested in it.

There are three main components that characterise a mutual fund (later simply fund):

- The fund's participants are the investors who invest in the fund's assets, acquiring shares through their capital;

• The management company, which is the management hub of the fund's activities, which has the function of starting the fund itself, of establishing its own regulation and managing its portfolio; and

• Depositary banks which physically hold the fund's securities and keep cash in hand. The banks also have a controlling role on the legitimacy of the fund's assets on the basis of the provisions of the Bank of America and the fund regulations.

The unit value of each individual share of the various funds is published daily in the newspapers. On the NASDAQ website it is also possible to follow the price trend of the shares of the various funds in exactly the same way that the trend of the shares is followed. The prices in question already incorporate the return on the fund.

There are various types of mutual funds, the best known are the following three:

• Equity funds invest mainly in shares or convertible bonds. They are generally riskier but tend to guarantee higher returns and in any case guarantee lower fluctuations than simple equity securities as they generally balance their share with non-equity investments such as ordinary bonds, government securities and with the liquidity held. Another way in which risk balancing is generally achieved is to differentiate by geographical area and therefore also by evaluating the fund's investments;

• Bond funds, these are funds that invest mainly in ordinary bonds and government bonds: this type of funds generally has the advantage of being less risky, but the disadvantage of being less profitable; and

• Balanced funds are funds that aim to balance the various forms of investment in order to obtain performance and risk profiles initiated between those of equity and bond funds.

Types of Mutual Funds

There are distinguished types of mutual funds – bond funds, money market funds, stock funds, and many more as discussed below. Each of these types of mutual funds has a specific amount of risk and return involved. Before choosing one of them, determine your financial goals and your risk temperament first. As a universal rule, the more the potential return, the higher the risk of loss.

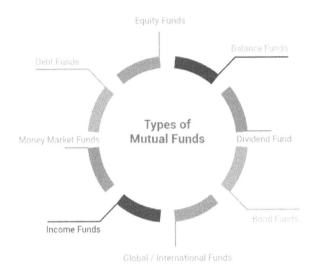

Mutual funds based on bonds

Bond funds include treasury bonds, insured bonds, and other types of bonds usually bought in the bond market. Generally, bond funds have higher risk and return ratios as compared to money market funds. However, bond funds have lower risk and return ratios when compared to stock funds. The major risks that are involved when it comes to bond funds are the following:

- Risk of the interest rate

- Risk on the credit

- Risk of prepayment

With respect to the risk of the interest rate: Remember that when the interest rates go down, the market value of the bonds will rise. Conversely, as the interest rates go up, the market value of the bonds will diminish. As such, should the interest rates go up after your investment, you can lose serious money.

With respect to the risk on credit: Remember that there are basically two types of bonds:

Bonds that are lower risk such as insured bonds and treasury bonds; and

The ones that are at higher risk are such as bonds issued by individual companies.

Basically, if the bonds fund you chose is composed of lower risk bonds (the first type), you will have lower risks on credit. The reason is that a state (i.e., USA, UK, Russia, Japan, China) is always liquid and will be able to pay its debts without resorting to legal remedies. A state can never be bankrupt. The downside however, is that lower risk bonds provide lower returns for investors.

However, if the bonds fund you chose is composed of higher risk bonds (the second type), you will have higher risks on credit. This is because corporations, partnerships and other kinds of businesses use various forms of leverage in order to grow. Due to such, there will always exist a risk that they will not be able to pay their credit on time. Should this happen, they will go bankrupt. The upside however, is that higher risk bonds provide higher returns for investors.

With respect to the risk on the prepayment: This refers to the risk that the bond might be paid off earlier than the due date. As an illustrative example, suppose that after you invest in a bonds fund, the interest rates fall. The implication of this is that the market value of the bonds which comprise your mutual fund portfolio will increase. This is a downside because the issuer of the bond will opt to pay the debt earlier than due and issue another set of bonds that have lower rates. Should this happen, the mutual fund will not be able to reinvest the profits in another set of bonds that may pay a higher rate. Instead, the mutual fund company will be forced to buy the set of bonds issued by the bond issuer that have lower rates of return.

Mutual funds based on money market assets or securities

Money market funds are mutual funds that are composed of money market assets and securities. Compared to other types of mutual funds, money market funds are relatively low risk. Conversely, the potential returns are also considerably low. If you are living in the United States, the rules when it comes to money market funds are as follows, according to the Securities and Exchange Commission:

Money market funds can only invest in short term investments;

Money market funds can only invest in high-quality securities or assets;

Money market funds can only invest in securities or assets that are duly issued by any of the following:

- The USA Federal Government

- USA state and local governments

- A duly licensed USA Corporation

More often than not, the returns (or profit) of a money market fund will generally reflect the interest rates in the short term. In addition, the returns of a money market fund are generally lower than that of bond and stock funds.

The major risk of investing in a money market fund is the risk of inflation. This means that the rate of inflation might outpace the returns of a money market fund.

Mutual funds based on equities or stocks

Stock funds are mutual funds that are basically composed of equities or stocks. Equities or stocks refer to the proportion of one's ownership in a publicly listed corporation in terms of shares. Publicly listed corporations are those corporations that can be bought by the public in stock exchanges such as the NASDAQ and the New York Stock Exchange. This means that the stock fund will pick a set of stock from a given stock exchange.

Mutual funds based on stocks are characterized by high levels of volatility, similar to that of equities in the stock market. This means that the value of the mutual fund can rise and fall quickly over a short period of time. However, research in wealth and finance have already found that investments in equities have historically performed better than any other type of asset.

However, not all stock funds are alike. There are also different types of stock funds in order to meet the specific needs, financial goals and risk the desire of different investors. Listed below are the 4 basic types of stock funds:

- Income stock funds

- Growth stock funds

- Sector stock funds

- Stock Market Index funds

Income stock funds are mutual funds that invest in equities that pay regular amounts of dividends every year or every quarter to its shareholders.

Growth stock funds are mutual funds that invest in equities that are found to have lots of growth potential. As such, investors would like to profit from these kinds of mutual funds through capital gains or capital appreciation.

Sector stock funds are mutual funds that invest in equities from a specific industry segment. For example, there are sector stock funds that solely invest in consumer products such as Kraft and McDonald's. Also, there are sector stock funds that solely invest in technology such as Apple and Microsoft.

Stock Market Index funds are mutual funds that invest in equities that are listed in a specific stock market index (in whole or in part). The goal of this type of stock fund is to have a return or profits that are similar to the specific stock market index chosen.

Income Funds

Another type of mutual funds is quite popular and is known as income funds. As the name suggests, they are used to derive a regular income and are thus employed as an investment scheme to end up with a fixed income on a monthly basis. A mutual fund never sticks to any one kind of investment and helps in diversifying your risk. So when it comes to income funds, the mutual fund scheme will not limit itself to just one kind of investment. It will look for several inner compositions for all its varieties. Thus, income funds will also be split up, and the fund manager will invest a person's money in all of its varieties. These varieties are given below.

A real estate investment trust is one in which the shareholders are paid a regular income for the real estate investments they make. This means that the shareholder is contributing towards the building and upkeep of real estate ventures, such as shopping malls, metros, office spaces, etc. Whatever the trust earns is split up and distributed to the shareholders. These shareholders will, therefore, derive a fixed sum of money from such investments.

Master limited partnerships. Master limited partnerships are those holdings where the company diversifies into separate subsidiaries. It will then allow the shareholder units that will comprise all the different subsidiaries. The shareholder will get paid whatever is earned by the different subsidiaries on a monthly basis.

Royalty Trusts. Royalty trusts, such as the U.S. royalty trust, pay their shareholders money on a regular basis. These trusts will hold enterprises, such as oil and gas. However, this type has seen a sharp decline in the past few years, and mutual fund managers refrain from investing their shareholders' money in such trusts. Government bond investments are seen as being safer options than private investments. This is mainly because they are sure of not going bad, and even if they do, the government will ensure that all the shareholders receive their money.

The main advantage is the dividends that investors receive. However, there are disadvantages as well. It takes longer to see any returns, as the profits from the investment are used to give dividends but not investment growth. Another important risk is the chance of interruptions, which means that the issuer, for whatever reason, cannot make dividends. It's important to see if this fund is worth the risk for you.

Balanced Funds

A balanced fund is a hybrid mutual fund. It combines three to four different elements of financial securities. It takes a few stocks, some bond or income funds, as well as a few market investments and then prepares a combined portfolio. The idea of a balanced fund is to help investors diversify both their risk and income gain. Thus, by having a balanced fund, investors can have a regular income and remain invested for a long time. Balanced funds are great options for beginners looking to increase their financial holdings and diversifying their investments, as these funds are very simple. They are very easy to understand, as this type of fund is just balancing the risks and rewards of investing.

The general rule is to have 60% as your fixed investment and 40% as your regular income investment. The choice is yours, and you can select a combination that works for you, but remember that there will be a minimum investment clause, and you will have to invest whatever is expected of you.

There is the option of changing up the portfolio mix from time to time. This means that it is not necessary to hold on to the same kind of investment for long. If you feel like a particular aspect of your balanced fund mix is not working for you, then you can change it to something else that works in your favor. This kind of freedom is not available for other forms of mutual fund investments. Your fund manager will keep you updated on your incomes and also let you choose whether you stay or take an exit on the fund. In most cases, the manager himself will take a call on whether to exit a fund or not. He will keep switching it up depending on market conditions and how the economy is moving.

Like all investments, it has disadvantages, such as the management fee being the same no matter how the market is performing. Moreover, it is not recommended to those who are in a lower tax bracket, as returns are very moderate, so to see a large return, you will need to invest a lot of money.

Equity Funds

Equity funds are another type of investment that the mutual fund encompasses. Here, there are three distinct qualities that the mutual fund manager looks at, namely, growth, value, and a mixture of the two. When you invest in an equity fund, you are looking at the growth of the company that you are investing in and their holding. This refers to how significantly the investment will grow over the course of time and what dividends the company will pay once it achieves a higher profit. Value refers to how valuable it will get over time or if it already is a big company. So you are looking for these both individually and as a combined output.

There are large cap options, mid-cap options, and small-cap options. It is entirely up to you to decide where you want to invest. Say, for example, you choose a well-established company that has a large business but does not have a good share price; this will be considered a large value investment. Conversely, say you invest in a company that has only limited finances hoping for a startup, but its share price is doing well in the market; you would call it a small growth investment.

The idea is to have some combined investments. All of them will add up to give you a combined profit in the end. The fund manager will suggest the best options that you can consider for your investment, as he or she will have a proper idea of what investments will pay off and how. However, as the ultimate investor, it is important for you to make a choice for yourself and not solely rely on the manager's suggestions. After you have done your investigation and understood which stocks will do well, then you can suggest these to the manager and listen to his or her advice.

Global Funds

Global or international funds are a unique type of mutual fund investments.

An international fund is one where the investment is compulsorily made in a country that is outside your home country. A global fund, on the other hand, is made anywhere in the world and might also include your home country. Overall, these are funds that are not limited to your state or region alone. Thus, confusing the two would be a mistake, and international funds can be considered as being bigger than global funds.

For example, a foreign currency investment is not necessarily a global fund. Foreign currency implies that you are investing in a currency that is not your own, but it is possible to invest in your own currency in certain situations. Let's say that a Texas-based investor invests in Japanese currency, and only Japanese currency. That means that the Texan is investing in a foreign fund that would be considered an international fund instead of a global one because the investor is only investing in one foreign currency, not including his or her own, which is the U.S. dollar.

The key to having this type of fund is diversification. You know how important it is for your funds to be diversified in the stock market. If you invest in global or international funds, you have the chance to invest in a unique fund that will give you good returns. You will tap not only into the potential of your own market, but also into the market of countries that might be financially stronger than yours. Now imagine having the chance to convert all your local currency into that of a country with a currency that is trailing. You will obviously come into a bigger profit.

These types of funds are popular but undoubtedly quite risky, owing to a lack of proper knowledge and inefficiency in predicting global markets. It is quite tough to tame your local market, and it will be that much tougher to tame foreign markets. Your fund manager will have to conduct a lot of research in order to nest your money in this type of fund. The returns, however, will be well worth the effort, and you might end up making double or triple whatever you are already making in your local markets.

Specialty Funds

A specialty fund is a type of mutual fund that does not adhere to the common description of mutual funds.

This means that they are quite unique and concentrate on a few sectors of the market. They can be classified as follows:

Sector funds. As the name suggests, pertain to those funds that are invested in certain specific sectors alone. These can include the technology sector, the financial sector, the health sector, fast-moving consumer goods, etc. All these sectors are separated, and the fund manager will decide to invest in the one that the fund manager thinks will throw up a lucrative output. The manager will not consult the client in general, as he or she will have access to the best information in the business. It is also advisable not to waste time communicating with the clients, as the markets are extremely volatile and every second counts.

Region-specific funds. As the name suggests, region-specific funds look at investments in a particular region of the world, be it local or foreign. The idea is to incorporate a foreign investment into the portfolio. This is achievable only if the person is eligible for foreign investment. The manager will have to do some amount of research and understand the markets thoroughly. There is a certain amount of risk associated with these types of funds, and the investor should be made fully aware of these before the investment goes through. The most risk to undertake will arise if the foreign country goes into recession.

Social responsibility funds. These are funds where the manager will avoid investing in companies that indulge in illegal businesses. These can include arms and ammunition building, import and export of banned substances, etc. If these companies get into trouble, then the investor's money will be in trouble. Moreover, it is the responsibility of the investor not to promote such trade for the betterment of society.

A huge disadvantage of this fund is the fact that there is a risk of lack of portfolio diversity because you are investing in a specialized fund. While you can invest in different specialized markets, it does not mean you have a greater chance of making a profit whether you invest in one specialized market or two.

Mutual Insurance

A mutual insurance company, sometimes known as a mutual insurance fund, is an insurance company that is mainly owned by policyholders.

The advantage of this fund is the fact that it exists to make sure that the benefits promised to the policyholders are there for the long term. This means that policyholders can make decisions that will benefit them in the long run. The main disadvantage is that members are charged a premium so the company can make a profit.

This premium is like an investment because policyholders have an option of receiving either a dividend or lower premiums. This is an advantage and is the best part of paying premiums.

While mutual insurance is not similar to either of the funds in this section, it is important to mention it so as to separate it from insurance shares. Interestingly enough, mutual insurance can become publicly traded if expenses have risen. In such a situation, all the policyholders will become shareholders.

An example of a mutual insurance company is Liberty Mutual Insurance, which is policyholder owned and covers many different insurance needs, such as home, life, and car insurance. It differs from the likes of MetLife, Aflac, and Progressive, which only focus on one or two aspects of insurance needs.

While this kind of fund might seem different from the others in this section, it is similar enough to seem important so that people will not confuse it with insurance shares.

Index Funds

Index funds, as the name suggests, refer to those funds that mimic the market indexes. Thus, if I were to formulate a portfolio, it would involve the various elements of the market index. It would be similar to condensing the market into my portfolio. Index funds are said to be independent and do not really fall under the category of mutual funds. However, for ease of understanding and practical application, they are added under mutual funds.

The main idea is to flow with the market and match its footsteps. This can be a difficult task if people do not understand how to interpret the market. The fund manager will assist in the process and explain the various elements that make up the market. The investor can then choose the different elements that comprise the portfolio.

The management fees that these types of investments require are much lower than those required by regular mutual funds, so they are a good option for all those looking to come into a good profit without having to shell out a lot of money towards mutual fund fees. The reason why these fees are lower is that managers are not as active with index funds as they are with other types of investment funds. Studies have shown that this type of fund beats actively managed funds over time.

Despite some of the advantages of index funds, there are some disadvantages. These disadvantages include a lack of flexibility because these funds are dependent on the stock market. Moreover, index funds, at best, only give average returns because there is no opportunity to outperform the market, as market indexes are based on an average of certain factors of the markets.

These form the various types of mutual funds that exist in the market, and you can choose one depending on your investment plan and how much money you have at your disposal.

Advantages of Mutual Funds

A mutual fund is professionally managed. It has a pool of expert money managers who research, choose, and monitor the securities the fund buys. Investors can diversify their portfolios by investing in mutual funds. Instead of owning different bonds or stocks, they buy mutual funds to reduce their risks of losing money. A mutual fund investment is also more affordable than other types of investments. Furthermore, it is easy to buy and sell mutual fund shares. Investors can buy shares from a mutual fund company. They can also sell back the same shares to the company anytime.

Asset diversification is important in investing. Every investor seeks ways to mitigate risks inherent in investing by distributing his hard-earned money to different investment vehicles. Diversification may be costly to a retail investor because he has to invest in various investments to attain a diversified portfolio. If he buys shares in a mutual fund, he immediately enjoys the benefits of diversification without necessarily investing a lot of money. However, he must check first if the mutual fund invests in a particular sector or industry only. If this is the case, this fund doesn't offer diversification benefits.

Another important benefit of a mutual fund is that it offers economies of scale, which means that the cost of a thing becomes cheaper if it is bought in bulk. A mutual fund is able to take advantage of economies of scale. Transaction costs are reduced, and the investor need not pay commissions for numerous stocks he needs for diversification. By investing in a mutual fund, less money is spent on transaction fees. Furthermore, an investor can buy mutual fund shares in smaller denominations. Therefore, he can buy shares periodically to take advantage of cost averaging. He need not wait to raise enough money to invest in a mutual fund. He can buy shares on a monthly basis.

It is also easy to enter and exit a mutual fund investment. An investor can easily sell his shares back to the mutual fund company. But, he has to check if the company charges any fee for selling the shares. Lastly, buying mutual fund shares is like selecting an expert money manager. The investor buys shares because he believes that the fund's manager will be able to grow his money.

Liquidity - The people who invest their capital in mutual funds can easily get their money back. In general, they can sell their mutual funds in a short timeframe without experiencing significant reductions in the market price. However, you should consider the fees that can be applied to your transactions.

Chapter 9: Where to Buy and Sell Stocks

Shopping is one of the most common forms of stress relief, especially among women. After a long, hard day, some women would go to malls and check out the new edition of makeup, shoes, dresses, watches, shades and more. There is an undying need to shop even if a person already has enough garments. Plus, trends and fads change from time to time. Preferences change and perceptions change. Which is why the market is a never-ending process of innovating, designing, creating, and discovering.

In this generation, buy and sell is the most common form of business. When it comes to the diversification of assets, most investors choose to purchase assets at a lower price and sell it for a higher price. The concept of buy and sell is actually quite simple; buy low and sell high. You can choose any asset really, from clothes to accessories, to appliances, cars, motorcycles and many others. It is solely up to you how to strategize in your society. But we will get to that later. For now, let us discuss the beauty of the buy and sell for investment.

For those of you who have high marketing and social skills, this could be one of your best investments yet. As long as you know how to entice people into buying your product, you are good to go. One advantage of the buy and sell is having a clean income out of your sales. If you are the sole proprietor of the assets, there is no division of profit among your co-owners. The only thing you need to finance is the capital you will use to buy assets at a low price, the shipping fee of the assets to and from your inventory, the necessary taxes paid to the government for registration if there are any, and the rent and overhead expense just in case you decide to open up your new store.

There are two ways to run a buy and sell – to do everything hands-on or to finance people to handle it for you. If you have a job and you have no time to handle the business, you can hire some assistants, probably some friends and relatives to help you buy and sell assets for profit. But if you want to do this full-time and establish your inventory at home, then you can save the salaries expense and the rent expense for other purposes.

Anyone can venture in buy and sell because this is one of the few viable investments with minimal skill requirements. You can literally work from home and gain profit on a regular basis. Buy and sell is one of the most recommended ways of asset diversification because it entails minimum risk and minimum cost. Of course, there are instances when assets turn out to be of poor quality. You can just make the necessary corrections and top up the price to gain more profit anyway. Another good thing about buy and sell is the wide market. You can literally sell all over the world given you strategize methods into catching people's attention into your products. Plus, you have a pricing advantage. So, even when you offer your merchandise at a lower price, you can still earn a profit because of the money you save from all other expenses.

Buy and sell has been revolutionized ever since the breakthrough of social media and the internet. You no longer have to knock from door to door just to convince potential customers. All it takes nowadays is Facebook, Twitter, Tumblr, eBay, and other selling platforms. What you need to do now is generate enough traffic to establish your name and products to the public.

However, you need to remember, like any other venture in business, buy and sell has its shortcomings and disadvantages too. When you decide to diversify towards buying and selling, you really need to commit your time and effort to the management of your stocks. It is not just a buy, then hold, then sell strategy. It is the process of maintaining your goods and merchandise on a good condition. This includes proper packaging, proper stacking, proper conditions of storing, and many other factors. Especially when you plan to buy and sell food, clothes, or books, these should be stored in a secure and safe place away from any insect or pest that might aim to compromise its quality.

If you intend to have other people manage the business for you, it is difficult to look for people who are qualified to look after the merchandise and maintain their good quality. You need someone who has the ability to scrutinize quality and assess the merchandise as a top-most priority. Taking the stocking procedure for granted can cause the ultimate downfall of your buy and sell venture. Another risk in holding stocks of merchandise is the probability of theft and spoilage. You know how thieves are. They are very cunning and effortful to get what they want. When they figure out that you have a storage area filled with goods and merchandise, chances are, they'll aim to pilfer what they can for their own benefit.

Lastly, as discussed above, the preferences of the people can change in a heartbeat. Storing only one kind of merchandise can be detrimental to your financial status especially when you aim to obtain a regular income. Sometimes, it becomes impossible to track the changes in trends and fads in a society. Which is why you will need a variation of products to sell. To do this, you are going to need a higher amount of capital to start your business. So, how do you do that?

Chapter 10: Indicators to Look Before Investing

Traders and investors in the stock market use different techniques to choose the securities to invest in. Some make greater use of technical analysis, others of fundamental analysis.

To choose the stock to invest in, especially if you intend to do it for a medium-long period, it is good to use both types of analysis.

The fundamental analysis makes it possible to evaluate a stock, thus understanding the real underlying value of the action. Technical analysis, on the other hand, allows us to understand which the best entry is and exit points from a stock and often reflects the evaluation of the fundamental analysis.

Furthermore, by combining the two types of market analysis, one can not only analyse the graphs, but also study the historical trend of an investment.

It is in fact important to know both the price trend at the time when you are trading and understand the changes in the past.

In this chapter, we illustrate the fundamental analysis parameters to be taken into account when choosing a stock and you will see how technical analysis can help you to climb up or down the price of an action.

Here's how to choose a stock to invest in.

As anticipated, it is preferable, in the stock market, to use both analyses, because together they provide a clearer picture for the choice of a stock.

Starting from the fundamental analysis, the parameters on which to base for the choice of a title are the following:

- ROE and ROA (or ROI)

- the price / earnings ratio (P / E) and EPS (earnings per share)

- the price / value ratio of the book (P / BV)

- news, management quality and visibility of the title

Let's look at each of these aspects in detail, so as to create a complete content that can guide even the less experienced in choosing actions.

The stock exchange operator who compares with the stock market to choose a stock initially looks to ROE (Return on Equity). This financial indicator offers the trader the opportunity to evaluate the rate of return on equity, ie the part of the financial statements that remunerates shareholders.

High levels of ROE, both current and future, indicate that the company issuing the security is able to guarantee a high return for investors.

However, the only use of ROE can be misleading as it does not take into account the level of indebtedness. By definition, equity is the difference between total assets and liabilities.

If liabilities rise, the denominator of the ROE will tend to decrease, pushing the overall value upwards. Operators then typically compare ROE with ROA (Return on Assets) which tells us how profitable the company's assets are.

High ROE and ROA values indicate that the ROE growth is truthful as the [ROA] takes into account the liabilities in the denominator that as the number increases, it will tend to increase, thus compressing the percentage of ROA.

The P / E and the EPS

Together with the ROE and the ROA, we also look at the P / E and the EPS. The P / E is the ratio between the stock price and EPS, like the profit generated by the company for each outstanding share.

The P / E falls into the category of "comparable", those parameters that can be compared with those of similar or sector companies. Some operators tend to compare the P / E of a company with that of the sector but making a mistake.

In fact, we cannot compare the P / E with the simple mathematical average of the reference sector, since the latter includes P / E of companies which, by structure and profitability, are not similar to that analysed.

It is therefore good to compare the P / E with that of similar companies rather than the average sector. So, when you do your analysis, be careful not to fall into this trap.

The EPS instead is the denominator of the P / E. If the P / E falls while the EPS rises is the ideal situation (assuming that ROE and ROA are optimal).

This is because it indicates that the share price is not reflecting earnings growth, thus showing an underestimation of the market on the security in question.

The P / BV

To give further proof of the goodness of the analysis, the P / BV intervenes (price/book value). If the ROE grows structurally well (like that there are no deviations caused by the increase in debt) and the P / BV is low there is a further suggestion of underestimating the stock to be chosen.

This is because the price is not absorbing the growth of the book value (equity) which is the part of the balance sheet that interests the stock investor.

The scheme to choose

To summarize, then, the fundamental analysis formula that allows the optimal choice of a stock is:

Current and prospective high ROE and ROA;

- P / E relatively low compared to competitors and EPS growing;

- Low P / BV (also comparable with sector competitors)

Chapter 11: How to Diversify

A valid question all investors ask themselves. After all, we must start from another question: why is it important to diversify your investments? Simple: to reduce risks. It goes without saying that investing in several different assets involves a better distribution of risk. So, if for example an action is at a loss, we will always have the hope that a precious metal is on the rise instead.

Below we will try to offer a comprehensive picture on how to diversify your investments, thus better understanding why it is important to diversify your investments.

Why is it important to diversify? We have said that this practice is useful for reducing investment risks. The world today is globalized, so even the stock exchanges are connected to each other in an extreme way. Therefore, the crisis of an exchange carries with it all the others. Furthermore, today's World, especially since the 1990s with the collapse of the Berlin Wall, has become economically very variable and unpredictable. The logic that drives diversification responds to the impossibility of knowing in advance the future performance of our investments. A variable in which, substantially, the risk of each investment lies. The basic idea to minimize the risks deriving from this uncertainty consists in splitting its investments into different projects, thus spreading the risk linked to the performance of individual investments.

Moreover, each asset is linked to multiple variables. For example, actions are closely related to a company's performance, which often, also hides its real financial situation. Such as in agricultural raw materials, in which a bacterium destroys the crop causing a collapse. Regarding the extraction of oil, just the disaster of a platform or a strike of the workers to cause the collapse of the flock and what about a coup or unexpected election results.

The main features of ETFs are:

- passive management

- their listing on the stock exchange as shares and bonds

With the former it is intended that their return is closely linked to the listing of a stock exchange index and not to the fund manager's buying and selling ability. The stock index may be equity, commodity, bond, monetary, or other. The manager's job is limited to checking the consistency of the fund with the benchmark index. But also correct the value in the event of deviations. The difference between the price of the fund and that of the benchmark index is in the order of 1 or 2%.

"Passive management" therefore makes ETFs very cheap, to which is added their large or huge diversification, and their stock trading. All this makes them competitive compared to investing in individual stocks and less risky. However, there is also a lack of speculative level, inverted, or reversed leverage. ETFs are very convenient as they allow investing in many economic sectors: liquidity, bond indices, geographic equity markets, commodities, commodity sectors.

Example of diversification of investments

Suppose we have a capital to invest of 500 euros. And so we decide to diversify investments in equal parts among the 5 assets. Now let's say that for each asset the trend was as follows:

Stocks: + 7%

Properties: - 6%

Commodities: - 10%

Precious metals: + 21%

Bonds: + 3%

Now, by making a calculation on the 100 euros invested per asset, we will have the following results: € 107 + € 94 + € 90 + € 121 + € 103 = € 515 total

We will therefore have earned € 15 or 3% on our initial invested capital. How is our result to be considered? It depends on our ambitions. If we play not to lose, then we will surely be satisfied. If we are traders who are content with little, we will be satisfied. If instead we do a more general calculation, perhaps considering an increase in personal expenses during the year, etc., then we will have a half reaction: we have not lost but not earned as well. If instead we are expert traders, then that 3% will appear miserable to us. Finally, if we are traders who want to push our earnings, then we will be completely dissatisfied. And we will think that perhaps having invested only in precious metals would have earned us 605 euros.

All this to say that the answer to the question of our satisfaction or not depends on us, from our ambitions but of course, also from our formation. In fact, if we are beginners, then it is clear that for fear we will tend to equally distribute our money. But if we have the right experience and training on the subject, we will have the nose to invest on one or two assets only and those we will consider to be the winning ones.

Components of a Diversified Portfolio

Before finding an answer, it is necessary to understand that investments are divided into 5 large areas:

1. Stock

Area consisting of all shares, funds, ETFs, individual securities

2. Real estate

This area includes financial instruments related to real estate

3. Commodities

For commodities we mean all those products mainly related to the soil, then cultivable. Like coffee, cocoa, sugar, soy, wheat. But also, to the subsoil, like the energy fields like oil, gas and so on.

4. Precious metals

Precious metals include, as you can guess, gold, silver and platinum.

5. Bonds

Bonds include both government securities and bonds issued by private companies.

Ways To Diversify an investment portfolio

Investing means making precise choices and selecting one asset rather than another. If I invest in share ownership, it means that I am deducting money from the other 4 markets.

However, it should always be kept in mind that money is something unfaithful. Because if today it is aimed at a type of investment, tomorrow it will move towards another. So, if today precious metals are good, tomorrow will sooner or later go to the raw materials. For tomorrow, obviously, we mean after a few years. So it's like a few years' engagement. But when he changes partners, he ends up betraying billions of people who believed in that area of investment. And every time it's a severe blow, because the values collapse

History is full of such betrayals. In 2007, for example, it happened to properties and shares. And the latter collapsed in 2000 as well. In 1980, however, it was the turn of gold. Of course, the stories of love are also prolonged, like that of the stock market started in 1984 and came up to 2000. Or like the one started in 2000 up to 2007 on real estate. Recently, however, money seems to have become attached to precious metals.

Therefore, money moves cyclically and even if it may "fall in love" with more investment areas, it will do so more clearly towards an area. How to defend oneself from the volatility of the market? Surely inquire and train as much as possible, reading the economic news, taking a look at the countries on which to invest (considering their economic and political stability for example) or growing companies. Then it is advisable to rely on a trusted financial advisor to build your portfolio together.

What are the best assets to diversify your investments? Experts generally place MTB (acronym of multi-year Treasury Bonds) in first place, although the state coupons market is constantly evolving. In this historical moment, it is preferable to invest small amounts over the long term. However, it is worth stressing that these securities remain the safest investment to date, allowing a regular withdrawal of coupons with returns.

If instead we want faster and more substantial results, then the stock market is recommended for us. However, it must be said that large returns also correspond to much higher investment risks. So, we have to ponder perfectly how much to invest and on which institutions or companies. The properties are still to be avoided, since, after the bubble of the last decade, they have lost value. Although, it should also be added that the market believes that when the price falls it is just the right time to buy. Just to get a regular monthly entry through rent. Or sell when the market is bullish again.

Bonds are another alternative but must be "guaranteed" and not subject to the performance of the companies to which they are affiliated. Finally, gold is always a good refuge, just like other precious materials or valuable paintings.

How to diversify our investments through ETF? Many investors believe, naively, that it is enough to increase the number of investments to improve the diversification of the portfolio. But this is a dangerous simplification. If we invest our savings in individual securities, be they stocks or bonds, the number of products to be included in the portfolio must be raised to minimize the risk associated with each of the investments made.

On the other hand, if we invest our savings in active mutual funds, or passive funds such as ETFs, we can achieve great diversification by reducing the number of instruments. Each fund (or ETF) is in fact a container of financial instruments, so with a few products we can actually divide our portfolio into hundreds of different securities.

Investment Portfolio Diversification

The optimal allocation you're your capital is dependent on knowing the risks behind each of your investments. Every case will be different and how you want to divide your resources is dependent on a multitude of factors that I do not have any way of knowing. The best way to know that you are allocating your resources properly is by matching each investment to the purpose that it is to serve.

Some portfolios are going to overall be far more risky than other portfolios. This is not a function of investment prowess or even income, it is far more depend on lifestyle. A single male with no children will need far less secure investments than a married father with three children. The single male will still need to have his secure investments such as a 401k, but his other investments can be far riskier because he does not need to support additional members of his household. In this scenario the single man should have different investment for each one of his financial goals, but each one of his goals are far less important than the married father. Allocating investment money beyond retirement might be a fund to use for extra vacations, or to plan for a family. One of these goals is more important than the other and each investment opportunity should reflect that.

Your investment plan will need constant revising as you move through life. Your goals for savings will change, as will your income and cost of living. Modifying this investment plan to take into account your goals is the best way of diversifying your portfolio. You do not need to slice apart your portfolio for the simple sake of diversification – as long as each financial goal is insulated and takes on the amount of risk you are willing to accept, then you will have a diversified portfolio that meets your needs.

Grow Your Portfolio

Diversifying your investments is a key part of ensuring financial stability. Chapter one opened with an example of using a 529 savings account to plan for your child's education. This type of account has great utility and many families will be able to secure their child's education but it does not serve a purpose beyond education. The investments you make need to be tailor made to your needs. The 529 plan only fulfills one aspect of what you need from your future financials. You will also need to plan for retirement, an emergency fund, and have more general investing money that you can place in riskier investments. The golden rule for diversifying is making sure that all of your financial needs are being met, and not relying on risky investments to pay for absolutely necessities.

The 529 college plan is a great investment but I would hardly argue its greatest advantage is the interest earned, or even the reduced tax penalty on withdraws. The greatest utility of the 529 plan is that it encourages savings be deposited each month for a long enough period of time that your child will have a decent college fund when they reach college age. There are plenty of other investments that could potentially yield greater interest, but no investment opportunity perfectly fits the situation at hand quite like the 529 plan.

Know the Risks

As you allocate your money into different investments, you need to know which accounts are safe investments and which accounts are riskier. There is potential downfall for every investment, but some are simply more unlikely than others. If U.S. treasury bonds lose all value, then the money behind the bond is hardly as important as the greater national crisis that would have to be at hand. The opposite side to this is planning on depositing small amounts into a college savings account and then taking that money to FOREX markets or the stock market to invest yourself. This type of risky investment could get you to your college savings goal but the risk is just far too great. The same goes with saving for retirement or your mortgage savings account. There are some investments that need to be safe guarded and others that you can submit to more risk. The risks you take need to match the risks you are willing to accept for however you plan on using that investment money.

Benefits of Investment Portfolio Diversification

Diversification is the process of spreading your capital to different types of assets to minimize the risk of losing money. Investing solely in the stock market exposes your capital to the specific risks associated in the stock market. If your investment activity for example, is focused on the automobile industry in the stock market, you run the risk of losing a big chunk of your capital if that industry tanks.

By spreading your wealth into different types of investment vehicles, you prevent one types of risk from wiping out your entire value of your portfolio. Here are some strategies that you can use to diversify your asset distribution:

• Investing in Other Sectors

If your portfolio value is still small, you may consider diversifying by investing in the other sectors. When selecting a new sector to invest in, you may use the method we discussed in previous chapters. Make sure that you learn about the new sector first and the companies in it before you actually pull the trigger.

Investing in a second sector widens your circle of competence. It increases the amount of companies that you can invest in safely. It also allows you to spread your funds to another industry so that you will be able to avoid exposing your money to one type of sector related risk.

One way to do this is by dividing your portfolio fund into two. You could leave one of the funds in the sector you first invested in. You could then distribute the other half in the new sector you've selected.

You could also go about it by leaving your old positions alone and investing only new funds into the new sector. This strategy is better if you are in no position of selling your older positions. With this strategy, you will be building up your fund in the new sector from scratch.

- Index Investing

Index investing is another strategy that you can use to diversify your fund's distribution. With this method of investing, you no longer need to spend too much time doing fundamental analysis. Instead, you only spread your wealth among the companies in the index you have chosen. For example, you could choose to use your funds to invest on the top companies in the S&P 500. You have a number of ways on how you can do this.

This method of investing is used by people who believe that it is impossible to constantly beat the market. This belief has some statistical backing. In the year 2010, more than 90% of fund managers failed to beat the performance of the S&P 500. The majority of the managers who did beat the market were in big hedge funds, mutual funds and banks that were only accessible to the rich. Because you are a beginner, we could assume that you will not be able to beat the performance of the market in your first year of trading. If you believe this too, you may be better of using the index investing method.

The first one requires a huge sum of money to get started. This strategy requires you to invest on the individual companies in your chosen index yourself. Pulling this off though can be difficult. You will need to invest a percentage of your fund on a company in your chosen index according to its weight in that index. Because the companies in an index are usually blue chip companies, you can expect some of them to have a high price. The board lot requirement for some of these expensive company stocks will prevent you from buying just the right amount to hit the sweet percentage of investment that corresponds to its weight in the index.

It will also be difficult for you to keep track of the changes in the index. The weight of each company in an index changes every time the prices of the companies change. This happens every trading day. You will also need to redistribute your own funds in these stocks every week or month so that your investment follows the weight distribution in the index.

If you do not want to keep track of an index and you don't want to go through the hassle of constantly adjusting the distribution of your investments, you could also opt to buy index funds. Index funds are a type of mutual funds that are specialized to mimic the distribution of an index in the market. Index funds are expected to have some fees though because they are run by an investing company.

To invest in an index fund, you will need to pick a company to invest in. You could then ask them if they are offering index funds. The best time to start investing in an index fund is when the market is doing well. Index funds tend to be of higher risk compared to other types of mutual funds. They are riskier than other types of managed funds like balanced funds and equity funds because of the tendency of its price to fluctuate. However, this higher risk is directly proportional to the potential rewards that you may get.

• Investing in other types of securities

If your goal is to maximize your diversification, you could also consider investing outside of the stock market. If your funds are totally invested in the stock market, you are exposing 100% of it to stock market related risks. As your funds grow bigger, you may want to put some of it in other types of securities. One option that you may consider is bonds. While company stocks are considered as equity investments, bonds are considered debt investments. The companies and government agencies who issue these bonds are basically borrowing money from you. The bond is the proof of the transaction and it states the amount of money borrowed, the schedule of repayment and the interest rate of the loan.

Aside from bonds, you may also choose to invest in commodities. Commodities trading applies a similar trading strategy as stocks, in that it requires you to buy low and sell high. However, instead of buying company stocks, you are buying and selling rights to certain amounts of a type of commodity (like gold, coffee, tobacco, etc.). These commodities usually come from other parts of the world and are sold in the US.

While the principle of investing is virtually the same, the style of trading is different.

- Investing in Real Properties

If your fund grows in value, you may also have the opportunity to invest in properties. Investing in another type of asset, one that is tangible, can increase the diversity of your asset distribution.

Investing in real estate though, just like any type of investment, requires you to study what you are buying. You also need to time your entry into the market.

If the price of real estate in your area is low compared to its potential value, you may choose to use it as your method of diversifying your income. There are multiple ways that you can earn through real estate investing. Just like with securities, you can also buy and sell properties. You also have the option of renting your properties out.

Chapter 12: Goal Setting

After dealing with your debts and saving for an emergency fund, the next step is to plan what you will use your money for. Allocation of resources is one of the most basic problems that the study of economics tries to deal with. This problem exists because we have a limited amount of resources and an endless list of needs and wants.

The key to solving this problem on a personal level is to identify the needs and wants that you want to prioritize the most. You may do this by looking into the different options where you can spend your money on and identify the ones that you really want to work for.

How to Plan and Set Your Stock Trading Goals

Let's start with the first step:

Step 1: Identifying Future Goals and Expenses

Setting a solid financial goal starts with your ideas. You may start by thinking of the things that you want to buy in the future. Most of us are already doing this. However, only a few actually do more than think about their dreams. Instead, most people only do wishful thinking and hope that one day they will have enough money to achieve their goals.

To start your own goal setting process, make a list of the things that you want to buy in the future. Some of the things that you may have in your list may be really important like buying a home or setting up a retirement fund. Others, like taking a big vacation or buying a sports car are not as important but they may make us happier.

After creating your list, put a number beside each item with the number 1 assigned to the most important goal. Here is a sample list that you can base your own on:

1. Create a Wedding Fund

2. Buy a home that's big enough for the family

3. Save for kids' college fund

4. Save for dream travel destination

Some goals have a predetermined deadline. If you have kids for example and you are saving for their college fund, the fund needs to be ready by the time they graduate from high school.

Step 2: Setting a Target Amount

When working for your financial goals, you need to deal with them one at a time. While we want to achieve all the goals in our list, we are more likely to accomplish goals faster when we focus our financial resources on the ones that are most important to us. When that particular goal is done, we could move on the next task on our list.

Step 3: Planning the Saving Timeline

Now that you have your financial goals set, pick the most important one and set the timeline for saving for that goal. By plotting the timeline, you will be able to know how long you have to save for the goal.

As we've discussed in the previous chapter, it's best to invest in the stock market only for your long term goals to lessen the risk. Pick a financial goal that is still a couple of years away from completion and set it as the target of your stock investing activities.

Step 4: Assess the amount of growth you need to reach your goals

The general idea behind investing is that you will need to make your savings grow so that you will reach your financial goals faster. You want to set the right expectations when it comes to the growth potential of your investments. Some of your trades will yield north of 15% while others will end up with losses. It is more realistic to expect a modest rate of return of 7% to 10% each year. Some beginners who make early mistakes in the stock market may experience even lower rates of return on their first few years of trading. While these rates of return may seem low, they are still better than many of the investment opportunities out there.

Knowing the average rate of return in the market, you will be able to make assumption on how long it will take for your funds to grow to reach your target amount. If you have $10,000 right now and you invest it and get an average of 8% rate of return per year, it will take you more than 9 years to reach a $20,000 target. You can increase the rate of reaching that target by adding more capital to your fund each month. You may also increase the rate of growth by taking high growth rate stocks in the beginning of the trading period.

To learn the relationship of the rate of return to the amount of time it takes you to reach your goal, use a compounding interest calculator. In this type of calculator, you will need to enter the capital amount, the number of years that you will be investing, and the annual rate of return you are expecting to get the final amount. Any additional income you earn in the market will be reinvested to it to create a compounding effect. This will help you reach your target amount faster.

Step 5: Practice with Paper Trading

If you find that the stock market is the best place to invest for your financial goals, you can increase your chances of success by practicing your trades. You can start practicing by doing trades on paper.

You can start a paper trade by taking a notebook and taking notes of the stocks that you want to invest in. You could then start by choosing one of these stocks and do a mock trade. In your mock trade, you pick the stock; you also identify your buying price and the volume of your purchase. Lastly, you set the conditions where in you will sell the stock. In the following days, months or years, you could then start to track the stock that you picked to assess the performance of your mock trade.

You could make the mock trade even more realistic by creating a budget that is similar to the budget that you will have when you actually start trading. This will prevent you from being reckless in your stock picks.

Mock trades like this allow you to practice with your trading strategies. If your mock trades often end up with losses, you may need to make changes in your trading strategy.

Paper trades also allow you to become more familiar with the market and the different events that are going on in the moment before you even participate in the market. It allows you to experience how it would be like to invest in the companies that you consider to be within your circle of competence.

The key to paper trading is to do it as many times as you can. This will allow you to know which indices, sectors and companies are most profitable.

Step 6: Get Started

Now that you know what you want to achieve and what you need to achieve it, start working on your financial goals. You can begin by saving for your investment capital. Ask your broker for the minimum amount that you will need to start investing. While you are saving, start studying the companies that you will buy with your initial investment amount. This will ensure that you will be ready to start investing when you have saved the minimum investing amount needed.

How Many Trades Per Month?

The costs incurred by those who enter into a mutual fund are the following:

- The entry or subscription commission paid at the time of the first payment.

- The management fee, on the other hand, is the cost borne by the cross-party fund manager. It is calculated on an annual basis, but generally paid on a six-monthly, quarterly or monthly basis.

- The extra-commission of performance is instead an optional commission that some self-financing funds in order to reward if, thanks to their ability, the fund's return exceeds a certain threshold based on pre-established parameters

How Much Money is it Going to Take?

As time goes by, you can see that there are other funds you can invest in and hold for a decade or so. If you can locate the right fund, you should do that. When a decade ends, you will be the successful owner of two or probably three funds, but you should not over-diversify your funds. You see, there is no reason for that. You can spread your money among an aggressive growth fund, a value-type growth fund, a global fund, and a small cap fund.

A tip: If you have bought a growth fund that invests in more aggressive stocks, it should go up several folds in a bull market scenario and have a spectacular fall, as compared to the general market during bearish years. The key to survive it is not to panic, but instead keep your eye on the years ahead when you will be able to make millions from these very funds.

Chapter 13: Risk Management

With the help of safe investing, there are some of the rules which you have to learn to have the investment safe and not spend all the money which you have hard earned with letting it go to waste. It is the fear which does not make most of the people invest in stocks because where there is profit; there is a risk as well. You may be lucky to get the instant benefit out of it, but you have to know these rules to be on the safe side.

Safe Types of Investment

You have to check over the type of investment which is working out best for you. There are five different types which are reliable such as the money market account, treasury, CDs, bank savings, securities, and the fixed annuities. With keeping the consideration understood, you have to make safe investments for yourself. You have to figure out the way to make sure that your primary purpose is to protect yourself and have the right side over these priorities becoming your strength. There are some high ends, and on the other hand, there will be losses which can be depressing to see the best interest for yourself.

Learn about investments

There are no safe investments, so you have to see which the safest one for you are. You have to learn about the risks which are associated with it to know which one is the safest option for you according to your situation. As there is no one law for you to learn about it, you have to check out the one which is ideal for you. There are many losses which the people may face along with handling the information which is not liable for them.

With the help of liquidating assets, you pay a massive return to the economy making sure the there is enough money which is on the safe place. It helps in inflation and brings the economy to the right place as well. You have to make sure that there is nothing left with the system so that your amounts are safe and sound at the right time. There are some principals which you have to follow to keep the purchasing power at the end of the accounts with the stock market.

Figuring out the amount

It is entirely on you how you determine which amount you have to keep and which you have to invest. You have to build the safe side and no one will be taking that decision for you. As the funds start to come up, then you can think of the growth, but eventually, you have to make the decisions which are worthwhile and see the results on how it proceeds further.

Along with keeping the determination of withdrawing the money, you can spend the time in learning through the processes which are the true projection of the needs required for the cash flows. There are some of the safe investments which you can depend on and be on the other side of the accounts to have the withdrawal for your fund which are available in the right timings.

Realistic Rate

When you have the returns in place, there are investments which are through the income and how you have to invest through the safe accounts. It depends how long you take to invest in it but if you are a part of it then there is nothing to keep in the mind which can be beneficial on both of the aspects which are keeping the investments away.

If you own stocks, stocks or mutual price range, you're answerable for paying taxes for them. The charges will now not be simply paid on the time of promoting the stock, but the fees also are applicable for the earning you benefit from them if the capital profits are going definitely so as your income, you are much more likely to pay extra taxes on it.

There are some situations wherein the taxes are deductible. And you've a right to claim these taxes. The maximum not unusual way to pay the price is the expenses paid from the investors to the agents.

By means of promoting the stocks after finishing 12 months will reduce the tax liabilities. Hiring a professional accountant or economic adviser is essential for an investor. In any other case, you may reduce to rubble all of the financing due to the fact these approaches are so complicated and cannot be handled alone. Now if you are going to make investments within the stock marketplace or have already got invested, you realize what to do. In case you overlook some factors, let's take into account it quickly.

Considerations for Safe Investment

You can additionally avoid the taxes by buying the stocks in a tax-deferred account. You are not chargeable for paying the taxes handiest at the time of promoting the stocks; you'll be answerable for paying the taxes in your dividends. Here are such a lot of options accessible, presenting a ramification of different pricing programs.

If there may be a virtual tour, even higher! Possibilities are you'll be making all of your trades electronically and now not actual man or woman, so ensure you're relaxed with that (maximum brokerages fee better buying and selling costs for a real individual thru their smartphone line to area orders). You should spend almost as a variety of time learning agents as getting to know the real stocks you will purchase. Ensure to observe numerous assessment websites that look at the accessible alternatives and discover the only that excellent fits your making a funding wishes/desires.

With the recent virtual improvements on Wall Avenue, possibilities are you'll be the usage of a web supplier.

The internet web page will possibly even provide a studies platform to get actual-time quote and in-depth facts on organizations. This will help you in studying your businesses and make better funding alternatives.

Chapter 14: Making an Order

When you enter into day trading, there are going to be several types of orders that you can pick. Some of the most common are shown below.

Types of orders

Market Order

This is an order to sell or purchase a stock at the best bid or to ask when an order gets to the market. A lot of traders like this type of order because it is seen as the fastest option. However, this isn't always the truth. It will guarantee that you get an execution but it can make it so that you get into or out of the trade faster than everybody else.

You should work to avoid this as much as you can. You really want to have more control over the trade than what the market order can provide. If you have someone else who is watching the trade for you, or you absolutely can't watch your own trades, it may work.

But it is better to go with a different option when day trading.

Limit Order

With a limit order, you are setting it up to buy or sell when the stock reaches a certain price, or if it is sold or can be purchased at a better price than what you set. This is the order that most traders will go with. It ensures that they get the stock for the best price and that they can sell it for an even better price.

Some traders won't work with this option because they are worried that if they use it, the order won't get executed. They think the program will just miss out on their requests waiting for a good price. With this order though, the program will be set up to place your trade at any level that you want.

Stop Order

The stop order is an order that will become a market order as soon as a certain price is hit. This is often a method that a trader will use in order to limit losses and can really protect the profits of the trader. You still need to watch what the market is doing and make sure that you know what is going on with your trade the whole time. Since the market can change in just seconds though, the stop order can be a great way to stop the trade before you lose too much money and can't do anything to prevent it.

As a new trader, it is important to know how each of these orders works. Start by studying the information in the first section and learning how you can use it to make a good trade. From there, you can place the right order for the trade that you are going to work on. Just remember that these trades are very short-term, ranging from a few seconds to no longer than one day. But when you know how the market works and pick the right stocks with the right orders, you can easily get some great results and some great profits.

Market Order

Market orders give out information about the best price and time when to sell or buy the stocks. It is not guaranteed in the market order that you will get the actual amount you wish for, but you will get the number of shares of your choice. However, in limit orders, you will not buy the shares until you are not getting the number of shares you want.

If you want to capitalize on the very best prices that the market has to offer, then you will make use of a market order. A market order makes it possible for you to buy or sell any stock at the best price that the market has to offer.

As a trader, there are times that you need a guarantee that your trade will be filled, and this order is the most reliable way to ensure that outcome. Should you wish to limit any possible losses that you may incur, use the market order within a market that you know has good liquidity.

You should observe the asking price as this is the point that you will fill in the market order to buy. If you want a market order to sell, then you need to fill it at the bid price. It is worth noting that the market order will not mean you have a price that is guaranteed. Instead, the fill is guaranteed.

Chapter 15: Stock Types and How to Choose

When the company is established, there is usually a small number of investors and founders. For instance, a company started, and it has one investor and two founders, so three of them have probably equal values of the shares. But as the company expands, it needs more capital for its growth. So the company sells its shares to other shareholders, resulting in the lower percentage of shares for the previous shareholders.

As the company grows further, it needs more investment, so the previous investors choose to sell their shares to make their profits legal. As the company needs a high amount of investment that a private investor cannot afford, the firm decides to transform the company from private into a public corporation.

Different Classes of Stock

Not all stocks, also known as shares, issued to or purchased by different shareholders are created equal. There are two main categories of shares: common and preferred. Common shares are the most popular and are often referred to as 'ordinary' shares.

Common Shares

Common shares represent partial ownership of a company and, as we know, owners are entitled to a share of the company's revenues, often referred to as 'dividends'.

The amount you will earn depends on the company's figures over a specified period, ordinarily known as the 'financial year'.

Common shares also come with voting rights per share; the greater the holding, the greater the influence within the company.

Common stockholders do enjoy limited liability but, in the event of the company's liquidation, they are compensated last after preferential shareholders and other creditors.

Preferential Shares

Preferential stock, just like common stock, also represents a share of company ownership. The first difference between these two types of stock is in the dividend share.

Preferred stockholders receive dividends before common stockholders. Secondly, in the event of liquidation of the company's assets, preferred shareholders also get the first claim on assets before common stockholders.

Preferred stocks earn fixed dividends, which make them more of a bond or debt than an ordinary share. Consider the following analogy:

If you give someone a loan, they owe a debt to you, and you will receive fixed interests on the loan. This is the same concept as buying a bond and receiving fixed premiums, or being a preferred shareholder.

Other Stock Categories

As a beginner, you will likely be dealing with common shares, but as you progress on your journey, you may come across other options such as the below:

Growth Stocks

These are stocks that have potential for growth in price above the general stock market price as a benchmark. Investors who purchase these types of stocks expect continued growth in the company's earnings, hence more capital gains in the long run.

Capital gains refers to increased price of the shares, hence the investor is in a position to profit from a sale of the stocks above the purchase price.

Blue Chip Stocks

These are the stocks of publicly traded industry leading companies in different sectors. These stocks tend to serve investors wishing to operate a moderately low-risk model, since they are safe and reliable, offering steady dividends. Most stockholders tend to hold onto these stocks for a long time, and many to perpetuity.

Income Stocks

These stocks pay much higher dividends than other stocks. Most of them have a much lesser rate of growth than growth stocks but are attractive due to the amount of dividends they pay. These stocks also tend to serve the moderately low-risk investor.

Cyclical Stocks

These stocks tend to follow the overall economy in terms of performance. For instance, in times of recession, these stocks will also fail significantly. Stocks in industries such as automotive and airlines exhibit this behavior.

Defensive Stocks

Defensive stocks usually exhibit the opposite behavior to cyclical stocks. They do not underperform due to poor economic conditions. Companies in the food and beverage sector, for example, fit into this category of shares.

Value Stocks

Value stocks are considered as underpriced by investors. These may be stocks with real earnings and potential signs of growth that come at a low price.

Speculative Stocks

These stocks show signs of impending growth in the short-term. Investors buy these stocks in the hope of making big profits as fast as possible. They best serve high-risk investors and aren't an ideal starting place for beginners.

How to Pick Stocks: 7 Things You Should Know

Winning tactics for different stock investors differ in the goals and methods, but a fact still reigns supreme: successful investors share common character traits.

Successful investors and traders have a higher intelligence level that enables them to collect and analyze diverse and conflicting data in order to make profitable decisions. In addition, they are full of confidence, as success in the stock market requires that you take a position completely opposite to the point of view of the majority.

Successful investors are humble. Despite the fact that they have the best preparation, effort, and intention, they commit errors and incur losses. Humility keeps one focused and allows investors to know when they should retreat and when to dare. Last, but not least, is the effort the investors must put in. That's how value investing continues to flow on. Studying the price patterns and market trends requires true diligence. You cannot just randomly buy stocks of a company and sit back on the couch. Exhaustive research of the markets and equipping yourself with the best skills are the keys to being successful.

1. Don't Take a Big Jump When You Start

This book is not intended for the millionaires, but for the people who want to start with investing as little as $1,000. If you are a working man or woman, you can compound your savings by investing in stocks. Even a meager $500 is enough to get started. You can keep adding more money as you gain experience and confidence.

The world is brimming with fantastic financial opportunities, but there is a need to learn how to recognize these opportunities and turn them into a successful venture. The United States of America has changed. She is now leading the world in technology, military prowess, computer software & hardware alike, biotechnology, and new innovative entrepreneurial ventures. The world is changing fast, and it is getting harder to live on a fixed salary. Everyone's heart is full of desires. You may want to travel around the world to see the places you imagined when you were a kid. You may want a home theatre and a pool to cool off in the summer, and an absolutely immaculate and highly equipped kitchen.

It is often not possible to have all this while dependent on a fixed salary. You have to create a second source of income. So, how do you create it? The most probable answer is, 'save and invest wisely.' The net profits you will make by this second source of income will help you reach your goals. Stock markets provides a lucrative opportunity for you to earn extra money, but the key is to master the art of investing.

2. The Golden Road to Success

There are no hard and fast rules to invest and reap profits. Everyone has his particular strategy for investment purposes, but some things are so common that they will never change. One of them is learning to pick stock winners. This requires detailed analyses of winners of the past in order to learn the characteristics of stocks that rule the stock markets. This will educate you on the type of price patterns that these stocks developed before shooting for the skies. A thorough study of past winning stocks is also necessary to take into account other key factors, like the annual earnings history of a particular organization, the amount of stock trading volume at different intervals of time, the relative degree of price strength that occurred in the price of the stocks, the quarterly reports that went public, and if the winning organization had launched any new products or procured new management, and how all this helped the stock to achieve it's enormous success. Let's take a look in detail for what you should take into account in order to find a winner.

3. Study Quarterly Earnings

While you are studying the past of the winning stocks, the most common thing you will see is the trading volume they have acquired. Sensational winners use to have a large trading volume before they start leaping forward toward higher price tags. Usually a winning stock shuffles around in price consolidation periods before its price soars. A significant thing is that winning stocks post outstanding profits. Their quarterly earnings rise with a wide margin.

John mastered the art of studying the past records of stocks. He shared with me the secret while we were vacationing in Florida to enjoy the summer. John told me that he confirmed one thing that any stock he wanted to buy should have shown significant increase in percentage in their quarterly earnings per share when its earnings per share were compared on a year-to-year basis. A good earnings per share indicated the inherent strength of the particular stock.

A tip: Earnings per share can be calculated by dividing any company's total after-tax profits by its number of common outstanding shares.

This increase in the percentage in earnings per share is considered as the most important element if you want to win in the stock market. John is successfully following the strategy. No doubt it takes time to study research papers and other documents that companies post online. The catch here is that the greater the percentage, the riper the stock is for investing. So, jump right in it.

John says that he just can't understand individual investors and professional fund managers and why they choose to invest in stocks that have flat current quarter's earnings. If there is no change in the quarter's earnings, the stock is unlikely to offer any significant profit. So beware!

4. Beware of Misleading Earnings Reports

When John moved up the ladder in the stock market after a couple of successful transactions, he too faced some serious obstacles. He even fell into one of the most common pitfalls - reading and believing misleading reports. He invested in Brownies & Co. after reading their report that suggested that the company posted record sales of $7.2 million, as compared to $6 million in the past year. Company's share holders cheered the increase in the sales. In the same report the company showed $2.10 per share increase in the stock for the quarter. There was a serious problem in John's judgment.

He did see that the company's sales grew 20%, but he failed to see that the earnings grew only 5%. That means John didn't get the profits he had anticipated earlier. He completely misjudged the situation due to an otherwise correct, but misleading report. Let me tell you what happens. Big companies get their reports written from professionals who know the trick of duping in naïve investors. John should have raised the question as to why did the earnings not grow at the same percentage that the sales grew. He should have detected that something was fishy. What I want you to keep in mind is that earnings are the real driver behind a stock's rise. So, don't be mistaken or fooled about it.

A tip: It is highly likely that a company's sale jumped by 15% and its net income, by 18%, and that is fine. Even really good. The key here is to read the part of the report that matters most for you. You are not the owner of the company. You just own some shares out of millions of them and that's why you don't have to focus on the net income and sales. Earnings per share is the key to success. Understand it and keep an eye on its rise in different stocks to make the most out of your investment.

5. Never Fall for a Company's One-Time Earnings

A company posts different types of earnings. Some are the regular profits that they make by selling what they usually sell, and some earnings come from one time sales of other items that don't usually belong to the company. John invested in a software company back in 2011 and the reports he studied suggested that the company made big profits and earnings in the past six months. What John failed to see was the source of these earnings.

The software company posted huge earnings on the back of a big sale of real estate that turned out to be a one-time earning. John fell for it, and the company failed to kick off in the stock market as John had expected. The company's reports can be really misleading. John learned the lesson that he must spend considerable hours on reading the reports instead of just skimming through them to see how much earnings it had posted as compared to the past period. The only benefit John got from the transaction was a somewhat bitter experience. He is all the wiser now.

6. Log Sale Weekly Graphs Are Important

My wife says that I am mad to study the quarterly earnings and the log sale weekly graphs simultaneously. Perhaps she thinks as both tell similar things and that I am wasting my time. But that's not the case. Log sale weekly graphs have great importance, as they show clear fluctuation in a company's quarterly earnings. These graphs just remove ambiguity from my mind.

7. Analyze Other Key Stocks In The Same Group

Whenever John opts for a new group of industries to invest in, he phones me to consult not only about the performance of the company he chooses, but also about the other key stocks in the group. It was vexing for me in the start because of the time he had to spend on two companies instead of one, just to invest in the one in the end. But today I realize that this forms a cushion against any possible fall. The catch here is that if you are unable to find any other impressive stock in the group, you have probably opted for the wrong investment. Better stay away from the group.

Beware of the companies that make undue delay in publishing their earnings' announcements. There is something fishy in the backyard. Don't lose your money.

To get a clear view of the stocks you want to invest in, read fresh quarterly reports everyday in the financial section of the paper like The Wall Street Journal. Some newspapers separate new earnings reports with up earnings and down earnings. This makes it easier for investors to streamline their investment plans.

Chapter 16: Record Keeping and Taxes

Make sure to keep all the data and records of the stock purchases sonic will be easier for you to claim the taxes. Always keel the copy of the document of the original purchase and the sale of the stocks. You can also seek help from your accountant about how to file the gains and losses.

While learning about the stock market, you will often find yourself overwhelmed by all the information in the market. You will need to keep tabs on all your target companies and the companies that you are already invested in. It is understandable to feel overwhelmed.

To keep everything organized, start a journal for your investing activities and thoughts. One way to do this is by putting all your decisions and your reasons behind them in your journal. This will allow you to keep track of all of the strategies that you use. It will allow you to keep track of the strategies that do work.

It also helps to used detailed notes that will allow you to understand why and how you gained or lost money. Aside from your stock picking process, you can also record your basis for choosing one company stock over another. Every time you invest your money, you lose the opportunity to invest in other stocks. It's worth noting why you choose to pick one stock over another. You may include the analytical processes that you chose to use as the basis for your decision.

Make it a habit to read your own journal entries. This is one of the best ways to learn from your own triumphs and mistakes. The investors in the world remember many of their trades. They learn from their past mistakes and, if needed, they adjust their behavior to make sure that these some mistakes are never repeated.

Manual stock management

Keep in mind as you read about the tools and tactics described in this book that you will have to make them your own. If you are more comfortable when you are in total control, you might perform more of your orders manually. If you're busy and doing multiple trades at once, you might automate more. Some of the analysis combinations we suggest might not sit just right with you, and you'll prefer a different combo. That is all fine! When you're finished reading this book we want you to feel as though you have all the tools you need to tailor your trading plan in a way that truly makes you happy and successful. We'll give you the understanding of what each tool and strategy really accomplishes so you will have the necessary knowledge to replace or substitute confidently.

It is important to watch these trades closely and be prepared to manually exit the position if the fund fails to reach the level of your take profit. Because you won't be able to chart ETFs on the same number of indicators, you will need to be ready to respond to unforeseen shifts.

You'll need to know exactly what makes a position attractive, what defines your entry point, what risk/reward ratio will set your targets, and what will cause you to manually exit a position. If any of these parameters are fuzzy or unclear, you will make yourself vulnerable to the biggest danger for any trader: emotion. It's easy to get fearful, proud, or thrill-seeking and undercut your own success. Having a clear, concrete plan prevents this.

Computer-based stock management

A significant percentage of buyers use technology — within the shape of online buying and selling systems that offer charting, studies, and back testing gear — to help them refine their strategies. A computer and software program can provide essential information about the technical and crucial traits approximately shares. But, many investors make the not great mistake of depending on an excessive amount of on this equipment without full knowledge of their abilities.

The Wash Rule

Whenever you sell the stocks, the taxes imply on the profits you gain from that trading. So you need to subtract the value in which you bought your shares from the amount in which you sold it. And that is known as the capital gains.

If your capital gains are positive, then you have to pay taxes for that profit. The fee is calculated as, if the stocks that you own, you want to sell it in less than completing a whole year. Then this type of gain is known as a short-term capital gain. And you will pay the taxes on it as the same value as your earnings. So according to this, the tax rates depend upon your revenues and the comparable tax rates.

And if you own the stocks and sell it after completing the whole year, then this type of capital gain is known as long-term capital gains. And in this type, you are going to pay taxes at a lower rate. And it also depends upon your income. The rules for paying taxes on long-term capital gains and the restricted shares have not been changed so much. The individuals in 10-15% of the tax bracket will pay 0%, those who are between 25-35% will pay 15%, and those individuals who are in 39.6% tax bracket will pay 20%.

So always remember this thing in your mind that whether you sell your stock or not, you are responsible for paying taxes upon your incomes that you are gaining from your dividends of stocks, mutual funds or bonds.

Chapter 17: Trading Strategy

Here are the four basic trading strategies that you should look into. They all involve subsidiary strategies. There is a lot of confusion regarding these strategies because a lot of people use different labels for them, but I have simplified them as much as possible into four different types. Many of these come under fancy names but focus on what you are actually doing. That is how I have classified these strategies to make them as clear as possible.

It is also important to understand that regardless of the strategy that you employ; in addition, you have to do proper analysis. Analysis is what will make or break these strategies. These strategies can help you achieve your financial goals on a day-to-day basis or a long-term basis only if you do the proper analysis.

Costs Inherent With Trading Strategies

There are two types of stock analysis. There are the fundamental and technical analyses. I will go into that in the next chapter but in this chapter, I am just going to walk you through the four basic trading strategies.

Swing Trading

Swing trading involves buying stock in a company and waiting between two to six days to a couple of weeks for that stock to reach its full potential. By full potential, I am not necessarily talking about the stock going up. If you are short selling the stock, its fullest potential for you, at least, is when it crashes to a very low level. Once it reaches a target point, you then exit the stock. Swing traders normally put in a good-until-canceled order.

For example, based on technical analysis, a stock is showing a lot of volume, and it is meeting a lot of resistance at 30. Based on volume analysis, it seems like people are buying more and more into the stock, and the volume is increasing tremendously. In this situation, I would then put in a good-until-canceled buy limit order for any price above $30. Sure enough, a lot more investors plow into the stock, and the stock goes past the $30 resistance level, and I lock at $30.25. It then hits $31 and there is a pullback to $29.

A swing trader would wait several days or even a couple of weeks until the stock reaches a profitable point or to maximize opportunity costs; the trader leaves the stock at a slight loss. Whatever the case may be, swing trading involves taking a position only to the point where the stock reaches your target appreciation and you automatically exit. Swing traders can utilize technical stock analysis using volume and price fluctuations, or they can employ stock value analysis by paying attention to things like the revenue of the company, competitive position, industry position as well as prospective developments in the news that might impact the company's stock performance. Regardless of the analysis that they used, swing traders pursue a strategy where they will remain parked in the stock for enough time to see a nice swing up or a nice swing down.

Position Trading

A position trader is somebody who will buy a position in a company for the long term. By long term, we are talking about several months to even years. The position trader is not really worried about the short-term fluctuations of the stock. This type of strategy does not rely on trends or market fluctuations in terms of the company's particular evaluation. Instead, the position trader uses a strategy that smoothes out whatever near-term price volatility may be. The key to success in position trading is a fairly long-term yet steady rate of appreciation.

For example, if your end goal is to protect your money's value against inflation and taxes, then your strategy would be to take the rate of inflation as well as your desired growth rate and use that as your ROI benchmark. You do this, of course, with the understanding that taxes will be taken up. So, a position trader then would look at the beginning the year when they bought the position and at the end of the year where they are still hanging on to the stock. If they see that there is a nice percentage increase in ROI, compared to inflation and other factors; afterward, they consider their trade successful.

Usually, position traders would not just measure their success against inflation because, let us face it, for the past decade, inflation has been very, very low. In fact, it is abnormally inferior by historical standards. It is so low that it is kind of scary if you ask me.

Instead, the position trader would factor in opportunity costs. An opportunity cost is obviously defined as the value of alternative investments. Put simply, if you did not invest in this stock and chose to invest in another stock instead, how would your current stock measure up? That is when you know whether you left a lot of money on the table, or you are actually doing quite well because alternative stocks are not doing that great. Position traders use the Dow Jones Industrial index or some sort of index to determine the relative health of their portfolio. If they notice that the rate of appreciation of their portfolio keeps up with the rest of the market, then they consider themselves successful.

Day Trading

Day trading is actually not even stock investing. If you are going to be completely honest about it, day trading is simply looking at technical signals or use related developments that impact a stock. For example, when your stock research software tells you in real time that a huge amount of investors are just plowing into a stock, then this should give you a good idea that something is about to break lose. People are buying into the stock in very high volumes. What you would do then is take a position based on a resistance level and if the stock breaks past that resistance level, you lock into your position. You subsequently ride up the upward momentum made possible by the increasing volume of trades in that stock.

Now, keep in mind that this goes the other way as well. If your stock research software notifies you that a stock is being traded heavily and there is a heavy volume in sales, this is going to put a tremendous downward pressure on the stock. You then take a position at a certain support level and once that support level is breached; you lock in for a purchase, and you ride the stock down. Once it bottoms out, you later buy back your shares that you have sold short.

Day trading involves very brief periods of time. We are talking a day or less than a day. In fact, a lot of day traders are quickly in and out of a stock in a matter of hours. Given the fact that they trade in volume due to margin accounts, they can make quite a nice chunk of money by simply trading a small proportion or even half a percent movement in certain stocks.

Again, the whole point in day trading is not looking the stock and analyzing its industry significance, its future prospects, new products, industry positioning, so on and so forth. No. Day trading is all about looking at technical trading characteristics and making a judgment call as to where the market is going regarding certain stocks. You then lock in a position and afterward you either ride up the stock, or you ride it down.

Value Investing

Value investing is also known as the Warren Buffett strategy or buy and hold. Value investing boils down to buying stock that the market has somehow someway overlooked. What you are actually doing is you are looking at a company that is in a really good position and should be valued more by the stock market. For whatever reason, its stock price is, in your opinion, below its full value in the future.

This is how Warren Buffet became a multibillionaire many times over. He has this uncanny ability of looking at certain companies that may be trading at a very high price already but looking at their balance sheet as well as their industry positioning and the health of the US or global economy several years down the road and using these pieces of information to make stock purchase decisions. Obviously, he is doing something right because he has become one of the wealthiest people on the planet using this strategy.

It is important to understand that value investing does not necessarily mean you buy a company which has a stock price that seems stuck. Ideally, that would be the best. However, value investing also means paying top dollar for a company that is trading at a decent level now with the confidence that price is actually going to go much higher in the future. You then buy the stock, and you hold onto it for a long period of time. Your success meter factors in several years of appreciation.

As you can already tell, swing trading and day trading tend to go hand in hand. Position trading and value investing tend to go hand in hand as well. These four strategies differ from each other, but these two pairings involve quite a bit of similarity. Again, when picking a trading strategy, make sure you factor in what makes sense to you, your needs, your immediate and midterm financial goals as well as your risk appetite and risk profile.

Chapter 18: Using Technical Analysis

A technical analysis is a trading strategy that will identify the best opportunities for trading by looking at statistics, like volume and price movement, to help make decisions. This one is different than a fundamental analysis because it is going to focus mainly on the charts of price movements, as well as other analytical tools, to help determine whether a security is going to be a good one to invest in.

A technical analyst will think that the past trading activities, as well as any price changes, are the best indicators of how the security will behave in the future. They are not concerned with the intrinsic value of the security.

Your job as a technical analyst is to try to forecast which way the price movement of a security will go. This is often determined by the supply and demand of the stock, bond, future, and even currency pair. Often, this kind of review is going to just look at the price of the security. Sometimes, it will include open interest figures or volume.

What is Technical Analysis of Stocks and Trends?

Technical analysis is a very popular method to use for investing and because of this; there are many technical indicators you can use to help forecast what price a security will be in the future. Some are going to look at the current market trend. Some will try to figure out the strength of the modern trend to see how likely it is to continue that way.

As a technical analyst, you will need to spend time looking over a lot of graphs and learning how the market works. You will specifically look at the price changes for your chosen security, but looking at other securities in that industry, as well as the market as a whole, can help as well. This can help you see patterns that make it easier to estimate.

To make your technical analysis work, you need to be good at reading graphs and understanding how the market works. Some of the things that this kind of analysis is going to entail include:

• Gathering graphs and charts about the market and about your chosen stock.

• Watching the news to see if there are any predicted changes in the market.

• Recognizing trends in the market as well as with your stock to see what may happen in the future.

• Making accurate predictions based on this research.

A technical analysis is a bit different than the fundamental analysis that we talked about earlier. It is meant to look at how the market, as well as the chosen stock, are doing right now price-wise and can make it easier to determine when you should get into trading for the most profits.

All of these strategies can work well to help you when you start investing. The most important part is to learn how to use each one, and then stick with it when you are in the middle of a trade. If you are able to do all that, you are sure to see some great profits with your investing.

What Does the Technical Analysis of Stocks and Trends Tell You?

When you are working with technical analysis, you will want to make sure that you are looking at the different trends that are going on in the stock market, as well as with an individual stock price. Trends aren't always easy to spot because the prices of a stock will never move in one straight line; they are going to move in a series of lows and highs over time. In this kind of analysis, you want to take a look at the overall direction of these lows and highs to figure out the general direction that the trend is going.

The stocks that you look at are going to either have an uptrend or a downtrend. The uptrend is going to be a series of higher lows and higher highs. The downtrend, on the other hand, is going to have lower highs and lower lows than normal. There can also be a sideways trend. This is when there is so little movement either up or down in the price of a stock that it looks like a straight line that goes horizontally. This basically means that there really isn't a well-defined trend for that stock in either direction.

In addition to looking at the direction that these trends are heading in, you also want to take a look at the length of that trend. You can have a long-term, intermediate-term, or short-term trend. The long-term trends are going to be the ones that will last more than one year. The intermediate-term trends are going to occur over one to three months, and then the short-term trends are going to be the ones that only show up for a month.

Trends can also occur within one and another. This is often going to happen when you are looking at a long-term trend. You may look at one of the trends that you see and notice that over the last ten years, you may find that the stock is going up. But in that time, there may have been a one or two month period where the stock went down for a bit.

We also need to take a look at a trend line. This is going to be a charting technique where you will be able to add in a line to the chart to show the trend of either the whole market or of the stock. Drawing this line is simple. You just need to start the line at the lower lows and then connect it to the higher highs. This doesn't have to be perfect, but it does let you know the general trend that things are heading in. These lines are going to cut through all the noise that happens in a stock (the price movement is going to have a lot of movement up and down, even in a good upward trend time period), and can help you tell where the price is likely to head in the future.

How to Use the Technical Analysis of Stocks and Trends

These lines can also be important because they are going to show you a different area of support and resistance, which can be great for helping you know when to enter and when to exit the trade. The support level is going to be where the price rebounds higher several times, while the resistance levels are going to be where the price will rebound lower a few times. The strength of these two levels will often depend on the number of rebounds that occur on the trendline, and they are important to focus your energy on a little bit. They can make a big difference in the decisions that you make with your trades.

And the last thing that we are going to take a look at here is a channel. The channel is going to be two trendlines that act as a strong area of resistance and support with the price bouncing between these two points. The upper part of the trendline will consist of a series of highs, and then the lower part of the two trendlines is going to have the series of lows.

A channel that comes on the graph can either go sideways, downward, or upward. But no matter which direction it goes, the interpretation is going to be the same. Traders will assume that the price to trade between the resistance and support trendlines until the price can break out beyond one of these levels. When this happens, the traders are going to start expecting a sharp move in whichever direction the breakout is occurring.

The point of working with a channel is to give you some really important areas of resistance and support for the price of a stock. It can really give the investor a good idea of where the stock usually hits. Then, when they see that there is a breakout that occurs, they will be able to do a trade based on which way the breakout occurs on the chart.

Technical analysis is going to focus on things in a slightly different manner than fundamental analysis. The analysts who work with this option believe that everything about the company is already found in the price, so it doesn't make sense to go through and look through all the information and fundamentals about the company to make decisions.

They will base their decisions on the trends they see for the stock's price based on charts, and then either purchase or sell the stocks based on this information. This method requires you to take a look at lots of charts and can take some time. But once you learn how to read these charts and graphs and learn how to really recognize the different trends that are occurring, you will be able to pick some good choices to invest in when you use the stock market.

Limitations of the Technical Analysis of Stocks and Trends

High frequency trading: High frequency trading is using computer based algorithms to make lighting fast financial trades, capitalizing on narrow spreads and selling moments after a sudden rise a penny stock's value. The capital requirements are very high and you will need to form strong personal connections with other like-minded individuals to get such a project off the ground. You can buy into an existing firm, and this is the most common way that many traders start working with computerized algorithms.

A high frequency trading firm works by collecting capital from investors seeking to become partners. They expose the money of new investors first, meaning that if there are several bad days of trades it is the new investors that eat the costs. The longer you have invested in a firm, the most protected your money becomes. New investors will always be the first to pay in case of losses, and as more investors join you will become more insulated. For payouts, it is the partners that get paid first, with the new investors being the last ones to get paid, and also get the smallest percentage. This might sound like a horrible deal, but the automatic process of this type of trading makes it incredibly desirable.

The premise is that a machine is programmed to make thousands of trades per day, profiting from the smallest changes in a stock's price. You will need to have a minimum of one hundred thousand dollars to be invested in a high frequency trading firm. I know that this is a steep amount, but this is an end goal, not a starting point. I include it in this book because it is the apex of day trading. Algorithms make use of all of the techniques in this book, plus many more, and make smart and fast decisions based on this information.

Short-term trading: Unlike many technical analysis trading strategies, this strategy keeps things simple. It is a short-term aggressive bull strategy that is proven to rise quite quickly on up-weeks while also providing gains during unexpected crashes. What's more, it doesn't require precise market timing as the earlier you can get involved the better.

The bulk of this strategy takes advantage of what is known as Post-Earnings-Drift or PEAD. It also uses the tried and true technique of buying in quickly on stocks whose performance for the upcoming year has recently been upgraded while avoiding those which have already underperformed for the proceeding year which is a concept borrowed from momentum investors. Another important facet of the strategy is to ensure that you only invest in stocks that do not include any options. The goal of this strategy is to avoid the more commonly easily leverage stocks in exchange for easier access to the desired stocks, with less manipulation to boot.

The selling rules for this strategy include a maximum investment length of 12 days. Likewise, you will sell if the quarterly earnings come in without any surprises, when the stock's performance drops significantly or if the earnings forecasts never start coming in extremely strong. The most important aspect to focus on is the 12-day trading rule though you may want to limit it to 10 or stretch it out to 15 days to cover either two or three weeks as you prefer.

Margin trading: Short-term trading strategies often prove to be reliably profitable in markets that are exceedingly volatile when compared to more long-term alternatives which will often see plenty of movement with no real net loss or gain. Thus, this short-term aggressive strategy becomes especially affective when it comes to short-rides on stocks that are on the rise. While this naturally means that many trades are going to fail to do much of anything, those that do connect are going to do so in a major way.

Margin trading is a blanket term given to the practice of using money borrowed from a broker to trade a financial asset which itself is then used as collateral on the loan the broker provided. The best part about this strategy is its potential to magnify gains, but it can also leave you with crippling losses if things don't go according to plan. Needless to say, it has certainly earned its reputation as a double-edged sword.

Due to these extra risks, margin trading can only take place through a specially cleared margin trading account which can only be obtained from most brokers after you have proven yourself to be a competent trader, broadly speaking. While stocks can be purchased through both types of accounts, most short sales can only be made within margin accounts and certain commodities and futures are limited to margin accounts as well.

Chapter 19: Advanced Strategies

You have to learn the best practices which will be in your favor so that you do not end up getting into the backend of the investment. You have to apply all the processes to make sure that you are on the right track.

Stock Exchange

The region in which you can buy or promote stocks is referred to as the "stock exchange." inside the U.S., there are three principal exchanges: the yank stock alternate (AMEX), the countrywide association of Securities sellers computerized Quotations (NASDAQ), and the new york stock exchange (NYSE), that's placed on Wall Street in lower new york in new york town. These various exchanges provide a place where shoppers and dealers come together to shop for and sell stocks, which permits for liquidity and helps make sure that dealers get the very best fee possible and buyers should buy at the bottom charge feasible.

Some essential steps for you to know about buying stocks to enhance your knowledge:

Elimination of Consumer Debt While looking to avoid focusing too much at the personal finance aspect of buying stocks, this is an essential first step that cannot be overlooked. There's no reason to be purchasing shares if you convey stability for your credit score card, line of credit, or another high-interest debt product. The inventory market returns on average 7 percent in step with yr, properly under the 18-22 percentage you're likely procuring the one's credit score playing cards. So instead of placing your cash inside the marketplace, put it in the direction of paying off your money owed.

Online brokers

There are so many alternatives out there, presenting a spread of different pricing applications. You must spend almost as a lot of time getting to know brokers as learning the real shares you will buy. Make sure to study various evaluation websites that examine the accessible options and find the one that fine fits your making an investment wishes/desires. With the recent virtual advancements on Wall Avenue, probabilities are you'll be using an internet dealer.

Depositing fund to account

If you do not have the regular bank account, then you can get the transfer of the funds to the separate ones already. With the help of the footnotes, you can quickly get through the larger side of the funds which are there for the deposits helping you to understand how it can be through the process and working over the more massive amounts.

Understand the types

There are various types which you have to understand to make sure that you chose the right path for yourself. Within the timely manner, there are current accounts which you have to pay for, and it will be working with you over the period. Know that there will be some types which may be working over the limits and within the time there will a stop over the purchase and the selling. With the market purchase, you will be there to help out the margins and keep them under control.

Placing the trade

Make sure that when you are setting the business, there should be additional information for you to keep in mind with the help of ordering through the first patch which will be there among others. You have to keep in mind that the trade is not there to be under the market order and shouldn't take more than usual to place the market price under the training option for you.

Monitoring the stocks

When you have complete control over the trades and how emotional it gets with the ups and downs of the capital you have to keep on knowing the pattern so that you are on the right track. The market and the investments should be done throughout the way with knowing where it is inclining and how you can find it better for yourself and the business in which you are investing.

Stay Alert

To be a well-informed investor, it's critical to get live updates about the opinions and marketplace events.

Reading on-line monetary information, blogs, and magazines is a convenient form of passive studies that might be completed every day. Often, a few weblog put up or news article could shape the premise of underlying investment studies.

For instance, analyzing some news article concerning the main acquisition may want to spur greater research into the premise that drives a specific enterprise. The internet does offer extremely good comfort level, wherein a widespread occasion might be analyzed merely via distinct perspectives with the aid of numerous investment experts. Regularly, an underlying argument can be essential like "there may be a movement far away from the poverty in emerging markets that are making people move into the middle bracket reputation. Resultantly, there could be an increase within the exact X call for." Taking this one step beforehand, the investor may deduce that together with the surge in the right X demand, the producers of excellent X could likely prosper.

Such form of essential evaluation makes floor for the complete "story" behind their funding that justifies shopping for a few stocks in a specific enterprise. An essential requirement of the studies is scrutinizing the theories and assumptions of the number one argument: whilst the delivery of suitable X is unlimited, an boom in the call for might probably have much less impact on the corporations within the selling/generating good X business. After you're satisfied and at ease of the essential argument after doing this form of research, the investor presentation reviews and company press releases are just ideal for the continued analysis.

Staying Patient

Staying powerfully patient is absolutely a distinctive feature while this comes to funding – in terms of patiently awaiting the proper time for coming into a role, and expecting some time until you have got finished all of the homework before making your first actual investment. The probabilities of achievement could beautify substantially when you recognize very well approximately what you are doing.

Quite a few long-time period traders typically use the essential analysis for locating out viable possibilities.

While you are inquisitive about expertise these techniques, examine fundamental analysis that might educate you the tools and techniques utilized by a hit funding professionals. You'll find out how to research cash go with the flow and income statements, spot vulnerable factors in a stability sheet of the inventory, and also use unique valuation ratios for evaluating possibilities in specific on-demand video, interactive content material, and physical activities.

Its bottom line is there's not a single way to pick stocks. It is good to don't forget all inventory strategies as not anything however a theory application– the "best guess" approximately the way to do making an investment. Also, regularly two hostile theories might be very a success. Likely, simply as crucial as considering a theory, is to determine how well the funding strategy does healthy your danger tolerance, time frame, private outlook, and the time that you have to dedicate for making an investment and choosing stocks.

The maximum critical and vital aspects of the inventory-picking: the essential analysis, a principle which underlies all strategies that we search. Although there're lots of variations among those techniques, they all come down to explore the well worth of a few business enterprises. You need to keep it for your mind as you proceed.

Chapter 20: Margin Trading

When the investors have to buy the stocks with keeping the investment in their mind that is when the trading account is used. It does hold not only the stocks but also securities, cash and other types of investors which the owner of the shares want to make and save too. The account is with the financial institution with the title of trading account since you are working with the stock market. It deals with the investments which you will be getting as an account holder and the strategies to make it a better experience for you. There are many different types of trading accounts which you will discover here in this chapter. It also includes the margin accounts and cash accounts specifically.

With those stocks, there are large stocks which can be recognized with the agencies having growth within the marketplace with enormous records. They're commonly paid as the dividends which can be classified within the other manner spherical. The dimensions of the organization have its market capitalization that's under the huge, mid or small cap thru the stocks. While the market is small, it is called "microcap" and has the bottom of the stocks recognized for the "penny shares." alongside that, there are no earnings with these companies which have high pay returns with the dividends which can be speculative at instances.

What Is Margin?

The margin trading account keeps a line of credit to your firm with helping you buy the stocks through the brokerage firm which also keeps the securities under consideration if you want to. There are numerous options to open the account with the margin accounts. You can opt out the possibility of buying the right purchase without listing out any price of a specific stock in the market. You have to consider, and without any complications, you will have the account with you to get into the stock market.

Margin trading is simply trading using money you do not have. You borrow money from your brokerage based on a certain ratio. You then pay your brokerage a daily interest on that money you borrowed.

Understanding Margin

When you get the margin, it means that the brokerage offers your o have the trading account. You have to remember that the purchase of the credit is needed with the new stocks in there. In this case, you borrow the money from someone to have the investors over the trades. It also saves the interested when you are holding the position with keeping it overnight with the interest rate which is over the course. You have to follow the dependency over the time with the slight usage of 2% and how it helps in improving the right side of the margin with allowing it to be the right profit for you which you could use for putting it in the market with the market all along.

Buying on Margin

The cash trading account works out, and you can get that one when the owner of the stock is using the cash from that specific account. Suppose you get about $20,000 which you have in the account, and if you want to spend half of it, then you will be considering this type of, so you have easy access with having the buying power as well. The only thing which you have to know about cash trading account is that you cannot borrow the money, so you have to purchase something which you are getting in the trade as a source of cash to be placed in the account. Brokerage will help you out with the transactions which are over the days to help you find the margin accounts so that you can get the direct access for the brokerage over the trading and keep it aligned too.

Chapter 21: Stop Loss and Take Profit

Another thing that you can consider doing is to set up some stop points. These are basically the points when you will exit the market, both when you are making profits and when you are losing. These can help to minimize your risks because you will make the decisions about these stop points before you enter the market and money is at stake. If you forget to do these, it can sometimes be hard to get out of the market at the right time, no matter how much logic you use.

The first stop point that you need to set is the one where you will exit the market when you are losing money. While you never want to think about losing money, it is much better to do this before you put any money in. This stop point should be at a place where you would still be comfortable with losing that money if things go wrong. Then, as soon as the market reaches that point, you will exit the market, no matter what may happen later on.

How to Use a Stop-Loss and a Take-Profit in Forex Trading

The ideal way to maintain full control of the price level on your chosen shares is to take advantage of a stop order. This order will help you to buy or sell at certain levels. If you have a limit order in place, then the stop order would work in the opposite direction.

With a buy stop order, the placement would be above the market price, and with the sell stop order, it would be below. When you have reached the stop order level, then the order is changed to a limit order or market order as per your specifications.

There are three main types of stop orders that you can use. These are the stop order, which is fairly standard, the stop limit order and the trailing stop order. While the other two stop orders are held within the marketplace, trailing stop orders are held by a broker until it is possible to complete execution.

How to Place Stop-Losses in Forex

Before you go into a trade, it is important to set up your entry and exit points. These are going to help maximize your profits like minimizing the potential losses that you could have. You need to have an idea of what price point the stock needs to be at for you to enter the trade. And then you need to have stop points for both ends of the spectrum for your profits and your losses.

Setting a stop point for losses can ensure that you only lose so much money. There are times when the market will plummet very quickly. If you don't have this in place, the market could slip down and you could lose a ton of money in a short amount of time. This stop point tells the brokerage account when you want to leave the market so you can limit your losses as much as possible.

You also want an exit strategy when it comes to how much money you want to make as profits. While this may seem silly as a trader, you want to earn as much as possible. But since there is a lot of variability in the market during the day, the market can often reach a high point and turn, without going back up again. Setting this point helps you to earn as much profit as possible without you staying in the market too long.

Examples of Placing Stop-Loss Strategies

Another basis that you can use in selling your positions is your financial goals. Always be aware of your financial goal. Each trade you make should help you inch closer towards that goal.

Let's say that you currently have $10,000 in your portfolio and your goal is to make it grow to $20,000 in the next five years. Since your goal is a 100% growth and you still have five years to work with, you can aim for high risk and high reward companies. This term is usually used for smaller companies that have a potential for growth. You could then exit each trade in these types of companies after making 8-10% gains. You will be able to reach your target amount if you enter the market at the right time and if you have the discipline to pull your money out when you get your gains.

Remember that as long as you keep your money in the market, you are also keeping it exposed to risks. You want to avoid unnecessary risks by exiting your trades when you have reached your goals.

How to Place Profit Targets

The growth investors usually invest in those firms whose benefits are anticipated to grow at the above-average rate as compared to its overall market or its industry. Resultantly, growth investors typically try to pay attention to new companies with excellent growth potential. And, the notion is that the growth in companies' earnings or revenues would translate into the high stock prices year after year. The growth investors frequently look for the investments in quickly expanding companies where the new services, as well as technologies, are developed. Also, look for the profits via capital gains & not the dividends – many growth companies invest their capital again rather than giving some dividend.

Conclusion

Making money on stocks doesn't have to be a big mystery. It doesn't have to be a gamble. By being clear on what your needs, are as well as the trading strategies available to you, you can put together a plan of action that can help you mix successful trades, not just once in a while, but basically every single time.

It all boils down to learning curve. You have to stick to the learning curve. You have to basically learn what you need to learn and take the necessary risks until you get the hang of it. Put in another way, if it was very easy then everybody would be a billionaire. Obviously, that's not the case. You have to stick to it and you need to put in the time to learn what you need to learn to develop enough expertise to at least trade profitably consistently.

Profitable trading, of course, means more than break even. Whether it's a dollar or hundreds of thousands of dollars, it's up to you. I wish you nothing but the greatest abundance and success in your trading.

I believe this book shared you all the necessary information you needed to understand stock market investing better and apply it to your investing strategies in order to become an intelligent investor and making money in stocks.

Lightning Source UK Ltd.
Milton Keynes UK
UKHW020636151220
375092UK00003B/316

9 781914 015816